To Mike Smit;
From Husban

Thank You For your support
#1 770

MW00938284

KEVON "ALACATE" HUSBAND

NOW WITH
THAT
SAID
JUST LET
THAT
SINK
IN

authorHOUSE®

AuthorHouse™
1663 Liberty Drive
Bloomington, IN 47403
www.authorhouse.com
Phone: 1 (800) 839-8640

Published by AuthorHouse 05/25/2018

ISBN: 978-1-5246-9397-8 (sc)
ISBN: 978-1-5246-9396-1 (e)

Library of Congress Control Number: 2017908378

Print information available on the last page.

CONTENTS

ACKNOWLEDGEMENTS

While this book is dedicated to the Readers I do have some special acknowledgements to make.

Firstly To My Lord and Savior Jesus Christ because without him nothing is possible in this life. My parents who instilled in me the work ethic to be successful. Pastor Renee Clarke the first preacher to tell me that there were levels to myself that leads to greatness. My late Grandmother Linda Husband the greatest example of Christ-like love I have ever seen. My late uncle Richard Husband the most gentle human being I have ever come across in my life. I know I made you proud. Allyson Holder that friend who always encouraged me to overachieve and saved my life in many ways. My Wife Letesha thank you for understanding, love and patience. The most Beautiful baby boy in the world my son Kai. You are my inspiration. Kimmie Joesph A real friend and an even bigger supporter. Ms. Dorothy Ham who encouraged me to keep on working diligently on this book. My great Friend LRich for being there encouraging me when

I was ready to quit and helping me to keep focused. My good friend Yvette Moreno you encouraged me when I was at the lowest point in my life. My Friend Nkesa for always letting me know I am loved and appreciated. My Siblings Devon, Shev and Janelle, Georgie. My nephews Juwan, Shieyon, Aaden and Amari and my little cousin Leishawana. My high school English teachers Mr. McMaster and Ms Reyes. Finally For all the people praying in the background for my success and well being that I'm not aware of.

THANK YOU ALL

``

FOREWORD
BY DOROTHY HAM

In our everyday lives, we are all surrounded by stress. Our homes and workplaces are partially stressful or even holy, constructed from some type of stress. We frequent eat, sleep and work with stress and even children are raised with stress. Even as adults, stress supplies our recreational knees in the form of sports or games.

In short, stress is so commonplace we invariably taking it for granted. However, stress is not to be taken lightly. Stress is the number one silent killer if not under control. The reason why most people fail, in my opinion, is due to some type of stress. People impose unrealistic restrictions on how they live their life. Most people emphasize on success/winning, they emphasize on losing, or they have the mindset that they are just not good enough. In either case, you are left with having to make rather drastic changes in your life.

In "Now With That said..." Kevon gives a wealth of information, ideas and support in his many scenarios, such as the story of "The Crocodile, and How To Even The Playing Field, and Life Can Turn Around". This book is full of riveting stories and scenarios that will captivate your attention for hours on end.

This book is an in depth look at an emerging at promising author with positive vibes to encourage you in your life no matter where you are.

This riveting book "Now with that said just let that sink in" is inspiring, encouraging and gives hope for a better tomorrow and a better today. Now remember, this is not a book in the typical literature mold. It is indeed a life-changing book without in the box thinking.

AUTHOR'S NOTE

"Now with that said just let that sink in" ….. A collection of my daily thoughts, life-experiences and readings designed to help you live a positive life. If you are like me you would have spent your whole life conforming to the status quo, being negative, lacking self confidence and moving aimlessly. One day I remember someone encouraging me telling that there are levels to myself that the world has not seen and it would be up to me to decide if I would display my greatness. In 2006 I made a decision to live a positive life but it would take me up to 7 years to see the fruits of my labor. In 2013 I worked as an intake specialist and with no formal training in counseling I realized that apparently people would trust me and tell me all their issues and problems. At first I was a little afraid but I started praying asking God to help me say the right things to the people I interact with. Soon enough I was becoming a positive motivational light in my workplace. People would come into my office sad but leave with bright smiles upon leaving. I realized that this is what God wanted for me to do. The bible says "study to show yourself approved"(2 Timothy 2:15) I began reading self help motivational books, watching videos of speakers such as Les Brown, Zig Ziglar, Earl Nightingale, Dr Vincent Norman Peale, Napoleon Hill, MLK, TD Jakes, and Brendan Burchard and looking up thousands of positive quotes and affirmations. I realized that I can take my life experiences and stories and use them for positive enforcement to help others and the birth of the idea to write this book was born. I know that when you read this book it will entertain you, put a smile on your face at last but not least help you to reengineer you mentality towards embracing a positive mindset. You will look for the positives in life and not the negatives. You will start seeking opportunity and stop complaining about circumstances. You will see the good in everything and everybody. You will learn own to control your emotions and not let your emotions control you. You will be on the road towards bettering yourself. My life was altered because someone spoke something positive into me therefore I aim to speak positivity into you. This book is for people just like me who have struggled with doubt/unbelief, Self pity.

Unforgiveness, jealously, Negative/ Pessimist thinking, Anger/bitterness and all the other factors that helped to create a defeatist outlook and fatalistic attitude towards life. This book is a collection of my thoughts. I know this book will touch and impact you positively once you adapt an open mind and heart. Eat, sleep and live positivity.

ALACATE QUOTES

If I was a magnet I would only attract positive –Kevon Alacate Husband

The standard you set is the standard you get- Kevon Alacate Husband

If you know better you will do better-Kevon Alacate Husband

Excellence has never been associated with conformity-Kevon Alacate Husband

Racism, even if it is in national interest should never be accepted, encouraged or regulated. Any nation that wants to look for an excuse to institute racist policies, is a failed state-Kevon Alacate Husband

Lines from a song written by yours truly" Two gunshot going to bring four, four gunshots going to bring more, more gunshots going to make anger soar, that is how you start the thing they call war –Kevon Alacate Husband

Aim for the stars and on your way up you will touch the coconut tree- Kevon Alacate Husband

Negativity is worst than cancer -Kevon Alacate Husband

At best a negative man can achieve mediocrity, however, for a positive individual, mediocrity is an insult of the highest degree and he will not allow it to be his life's outcome. - Kevon Alacate Husband

Change is free but development is what comes at a cost but it is a worthy expenditure to have. - Kevon Alacate Husband

You want to make a difference in the world? Then love the person that looks different from you, thinks different from you, voted different from you, acknowledges a God different from you, talks with a different accent or language from you.-Kevon Alacate Husband

Men seek out differences rather than seek out similarities so that they can act based on their prejudices- Kevon Alacate Husband

First rule of success...You were born to create, not to compete with others. Remember this.-Kevon Alacate Husband

Talking positive but living negative is like trying to drink coffee with a fork-Kevon Alacate Husband

Something I have realized in my life is that no matter how good my friendships are I will never agree on everything with everyone. I'm totally unbothered and cool with it. It's okay to disagree sometimes. No two people are 100% alike.-Kevon Alacate Husband

The difference between the successful people and the failures is time. Successful people will put in extra time.-Kevon Alacate Husband

If you think you can you will. Impossibility is just a self imposed limitation based on an inferior mindset- Kevon Alacate Husband

When desire meets knowledge and imagination it leads to creative innovation. - Kevon Alacate Husband

Alacate note.... "I remember when I was in college and I had to survive on the bare minimum, I would go to students' club just to get something to eat, I was working part time at a call center, doing an internship, late nights studying, get home at like 1 a.m. in the morning ..... I look back at it now and I appreciate my struggle because it has helped me to be a better person".

The problem with me and mathematics is that I never wanted a negative answer for any equation; I never wanted to deal with anything negative-Kevon Alacate Husband

Alacate note....." for those of you who remember when I fractured my both arms earlier in the year I was on work and some of my co-workers started rumors implicating that I was faking my injury... I'm not bothered by them but I decided to share this with you because I want you to know that I too run the gauntlet just like everyone else and I am no exception to being the hurled, the untruths and negativity. However I continued to stay positive, mind my business and don't let anyone's words destroy me" #inspiration #staypositive

If you believe you are blessed because you have material wealth I think you just might have missed the point of blessings -Kevon Alacate Husband

Planning without execution of the plan is like playing basketball without the ball. -Kevon Alacate Husband

To begin the process of becoming a better person you must realize you are not perfect, and then construct a plan to work on yourself to become a better person. Finally, execute that plan to become a better person -Kevon Alacate Husband

The only negative in life I want to deal with is camera film -Kevon Alacate Husband

When you believe, do so wholeheartedly and undoubtedly-Kevon Alacate Husband

Knowledge doesn't come from books but it is obtained from life's lessons -Kevon Alacate Husband

It is never just about you. I hope you remember that -Kevon Alacate Husband

Cowards are motivated by fear but the optimist is motivated by the end result -Kevon Alacate Husband

It makes no sense to get turned up in the club with liquor, drugs and partying and then get turned down in life because of a lack of education and ambition"- Kevon Alacate Husband

I want to be that person who tells the other person "don't give up, you can do it - Kevon Alacate Husband

Alacate note "I remember when people used to try to belittle me, I felt bad until one day I just totally rejected their notion and interpretation of me. Ever since my life has never been the same."

A smart person obtains an education but a wise person seeks more knowledge than the one obtained within school walls - Kevon Alacate Husband

I don't know how to deal with haters because I never listen to anyone who hates on my goals, dreams and ambitions. They don't exist to me."-Kevon Alacate Husband

Other people's opinions about your journey isn't your concern"- Kevon Alacate Husband

There is a dif0ference between education, information and knowledge: Education is what we are taught in schools, Information is facts and stats provided or learned about something, someone or some topic and knowledge is the application of education and ability to use information; to have the wisdom to know when it is relevant and when it is not. - Kevon Alacate Husband

Fears and dreams cannot share the same head space- Kevon Alacate Husband

Failure doesn't occur when you don't succeed, Failure occurs when you stop trying -Kevon Alacate Husband

If you're going to talk bad about me, my life, my projects at least spell my name right – Kevon Alacate Husband

Never try to impress those who hate your progress and success. As matter of fact never try to impress anyone who hates on anything period - Kevon Alacate Husband

People will talk regardless of what you do, so keep on doing what you are doing and let them keep talking. Usually the people with the least accomplishments have the most to say. Those that are trying to accomplish something have not much to say because they are too busy working to achieve something - <u>Kevon Alacate Husband</u>

Alacate note -"So you spend all day by the liquor store, sit on the stool drinking a 40, holla at every female passing by, refuse to go to school or get a job, then you ask someone for a dollar and you get mad when they refuse. Wow! Society. I'm sorry for the females that have to pick a husband out of this bunch"

Alacate note "to the wise the word "Love" is not a noun but it is a verb because it is suppose to be a doing/action word"

Sometimes you just need to do the mature thing. It's not always to get even- <u>Kevon Alacate Husband</u>

Never take the easy way out -<u>Kevon Alacate Husband</u>

Believe in yourself and in your dreams because they are the brainchild of your imagination and represent the conceptualization of your thinking -<u>Kevon Alacate Husband</u>

I respect everyone right to live peacefully regardless of national origin - <u>Kevon Alacate Husband</u>

In this life no matter what you do or say you will never be able to please some people. When it gets to that point you have to remember you're not here to impress anyone, just do you - Kevon Alacate Husband

Never engage social pessimists in any sort of conversation. It is never worth your time -Kevon Alacate Husband

Age and lifespan are not determining factors when setting goals. Passion and dedication are -Kevon Alacate Husband

Negativity is like influenza. If you hang around the wrong people you will eventually catch it - Kevon Alacate Husband

Rid yourself of useless, unproductive and negative thinking and introduce your mind to a new world of positive thoughts and limitless possibilities -Kevon Alacate Husband

Negativity is like potholes … because if you don't avoid them they will eventually take a toll on you -Kevon Alaca93te Husband

Whatever direction progress is in that's where I am heading –Kevon Alacate Husband

I dare anyone to show me one situation where being negative and lacking confidence and faith have ever helped anyone to be successful - Kevon Alacate Husband

When people misinterpret what you are trying to say it is good communication principle to try to clarify yourself.... however when people are committed to misinterpreting what you say and they claim that you are saying something you are not, never try to explain yourself to them. Fools never like correction and are deceived by the error of their ways and thinking - Kevon Alacate Husband

If you think someone is stupid or you resort to name calling because their opinion is different from yours, you might be the one with the issue –Kevon Alacate Husband

When you make a change in your lifestyle whether it is good or bad, you must also be prepared for the after effects that come along with it; so choose your path wisely -Kevon Alacate Husband

Focus your mind on positive things and go out and achieve them -Kevon Alacate Husband

Never associate with negativity -Kevon Alacate Husband

Humility is one of the greatest traits a human being can have –Kevon Alacate Husband

Regardless of what you think, your kids are a reflection of you, so make sure the reflection is good - Kevon Alacate Husband

Anytime you decide your primary emotion is hate you will eventually become overwhelmed with it. -<u>Kevon Alacate Husband</u>

Progress is never ending. Good is good but good is not good when better is possible -<u>Kevon Alacate Husband</u>

Alacate note "so I am in the car about 2 days ago and for some reason the key won't turn (this went on for like 15 mines). About 5 years ago I would have gotten frustrated, angry and maybe even said some "green" adverbs, but this time I just laughed it off and turned the wheel and then the key turned ... point being patience is a virtue, which we should all require and desire in our lives. Patience is always tested. When I talk about staying positive I always try to apply it to my life."

Learning is constant and that all I have to say about that -<u>Kevon Alacate Husband</u>

Alacate note "The ways of society is weird. So you reject a creator who loves you to worship the created that doesn't give a crap about you. Talk about an enigma"

The biggest and most pressing mental health issue which exists is racism. If you disagree, please show me one person who was a racist from birth –<u>Kevon Alacate Husband</u>

While compliments are nice don't be sad if you don't get them. Accomplishments are much more valuable than compliments -<u>Kevon Alacate Husband</u>

Always move on, never forget, most importantly forgiveness is not for the other person, it's for you -<u>Kevon Alacate Husband</u>

Don't worry about fitting in, instead you should always stand out. You are different and special"-<u>Kevon Alacate Husband</u>

Just in case you forgot let me remind you everything about you is unique and original. Always remember that -<u>Kevon Alacate Husband</u>

Not because you are someone's friend doesn't mean that person is your friend -<u>Kevon Alacate Husband</u>

Whether we want to admit it or not broken homes is one of the reasons for some of society's problems. - <u>Kevon Alacate Husband</u>

Respect to all the fathers in society who have respect for their children's mother and Respect to all the mothers who respect the children's father. Even though they are not together they understand the simple dynamic that children need to have both parents in their lives in a functional capacity - <u>Kevon Alacate Husband</u>

I'm not a perfectionist but I'm a believer in maximum effort. That shows your dedication and belief in what you are trying to accomplish -Kevon Alacate Husband

It doesn't matter who you are. Everyone has a social responsibility. That is what makes us human. –Kevon Alacate Husband

God's calling for your life is your calling. Don't allow anyone to claim your life and deceive you with their calling for your life - Kevon Alacate Husband

Before you can fix the society's problems, how about you first fix your own household problem - Kevon Alacate Husband

Don't be fooled …Liquor deceives everyone -Kevon Alacate Husband

People will be your friend until you start making progress, then you become their enemy all because you made progress - Kevin Alacate Husband

A dream leads to a desire, A desire leads to a passion, passion leads to determination, determination leads to perseverance, perseverance leads to progress, progress leads to accomplishment, accomplishment leads to Self-Actualization" - Kevon Alacate Husband

Character is more valuable than reputation any day of the week -<u>Kevon Alacate Husband</u>

Without common sense, book sense makes no sense -<u>Kevon Alacate Husband</u>

Keeping on working on your dream or else you will keep on working for someone else's dream"-<u>Kevon Alacate Husband</u>

Alacate note –"Unhappiness 101 – First step to being unhappy – Try to please everyone"

Alacate note –"Unhappiness 102- Second step to being unhappy – Dislike everyone and everything. Just be bitter, jealous and have malice in your heart"

Alacate note- "Unhappiness 103- Listen to every source of gossip and treat it like it is the truth. Also spread it so others can know of this gossip"

Alacate note- "Unhappiness 104- Never take criticism from anybody. You are always right in your actions hence no need for positive criticism"

Alacate note- "Unhappiness 105- Always be that person who believes that everyone has bad intentions towards them. Believe everyone wants to disrespect you and every conversation you have you always pick arguments"

Alacate note- Unhappiness 106 – "Never humble yourself. Believe everyone is beneath you and you are too big to learn anything"

Alacate note- Unhappiness 107 –"Always keep comparing yourself to people."

Don't Allow people to having controlling interest in your life when they never input any investment into your well-being –<u>Kevon Alacate Husband</u>

If they disrespect you, walk away. Cause if you don't they will continue to take you for granted and never give you due respect. Deny them the pleasure of your friendship -<u>Kevon Alacate Husband</u>

If Intelligence was to spread faster than ignorance the world would be a better place -<u>Kevon Alacate Husband</u>

Alacate note-"Dear parents, if you wait until your kids are in handcuffs in the court room to tell them you love them you have missed the point of love"

Your worst enemy and best ally is between your ears -<u>Kevon Alacate Husband</u>

Good character and morals go a long way towards establishing integrity -<u>Kevon Alacate Husband</u>

When your confidence level is so high, you just might be able to bottle it and sell it to others -Kevon Alacate Husband

Alacate note-"When someone tells you they love you watch and see how they treat themselves. E.g. If they use drugs, Get drunk constantly, smoke cigarettes etc…. that is a good indication that they don't appreciate their own body. How can they love you and they can't even treat their own body right. Don't be deceived"

Sometimes God provides opportunities for us but we get so caught up in our regular routine that we don't embrace the opportunity - Kevon Alacate Husband

Until you change your thinking nothing in your life will change -Kevon Alacate Husband

If you don't want anybody to know your business then don't tell anybody your business - Kevon Alacate Husband

If being broke and having financial constraints do not motivate you to want better in life, nothing will -Kevon Alacate Husband

Let the critics talk, they aren't experts on your struggle hence their words are irrelevant and incoherent - Kevon Alacate Husband

Every day is a new chance from God -Kevon Alacate Husband

The ability to ignore is greater than the ability to respond –<u>Kevon Alacate Husband</u>

Everyone is influenced by something or someone. Also everyone is influencing something or someone. There is never a moment when influencing does not take place in our lives. Therefore, be careful of what and who you are influenced by and what and who you are influencing - <u>Kevon Alacate Husband</u>

Focus on your goals; don't focus on the hate that comes your way, that's not your concern - <u>Kevon Alacate Husband</u>

Whether it is good or bad, those with a common purpose keep company with each other. Who is the company you keep? –<u>Kevon Alacate Husband</u>

Our differences and uniqueness are not the reasons to divide us, however, our interpretation and reaction to differences is what divides us -<u>Kevon Alacate Husband</u>

If you have to hate something then hate negativity, injustice, poverty, racism, war, greed, ignorance, corruption, drugs, crime, exploitation, tyranny, disease etc... I hope you catch my drift - <u>Kevon Alacate Husband</u>

If you need to make someone feel bad just because you're broken emotionally, then you are a sad individual on the inside -Kevon Alacate Husband

My definition of war is a process by which young men are sent to die and old men reap the benefits - Kevon Alacate Husband

If you spend as much time complaining than actually looking for solutions then what is the point of your complaint? – Kevon Alacate Husband

We must never endorse or condone wrong doing. When we start doing that your moral complex is beginning to disintegrate - Kevon Alacate Husband

The immoral option should never be considered –Kevon Alacate Husband

Stay away from people who are militant with their beliefs. That kind of thinking usually starts cults, terror organizations and groups which are counter-productive to society - Kevon Alacate Husband

This is a sad truth in today's world. Not because it is legal makes it right and not because it is illegal makes it wrong -Kevon Alacate Husband

Show allegiance to God, yourself and your family and let every other person or institution show allegiance to you before you show it to them - Kevon Alacate Husband

Don't let procrastination hinder your progress -Kevon Alacate Husband

You can't win when you are already thinking that you are going to lose - Kevon Alacate Husband

I look at the world and I am expectantly sad but not disappointed -Kevon Alacate Husband

Forgive people but never reward anything wrong or evil - Kevon Alacate Husband

When people assume things about you it is not your duty to explain anything to them. Their assumptions are not even remotely your concern - Kevon Alacate Husband

Motivation just like deodorant is not permanent. I strongly recommend daily doses of both -Kevon Alacate Husband

This world values diamonds which are none essential to us more than cleaning drinking water which is essential for life- Kevon Alacate Husband

Haters will hate. Leave them let them hate and you continue being great-Kevon Alacate Husband

If you going to eat an elephant you have to take small bites. Accomplishing great task starts with achieving small- Kevon Alacate Husband

If you want your life to change you have to change your lifestyle- Kevon Alacate Husband

If you must become an addict then be addicted to morality, success and honesty-Kevon Alacate Husband

Motivation just like deodorant is not permanent. I strongly recommend daily doses of both -Kevon Alacate Husband

The reason for Murder is a lack of respect for God. If one respects God they will not kill the creator's creations -Kevon Alacate Husband

Luxury goods were created for people who live in a luxurious lifestyle. When working class people buy luxury goods it's just bad economics - Kevon Alacate Husband

Don't let people change who you are. Anytime you make a change, it should be your decision and for the better-Kevon Alacate Husband

Racism is the descendant of Ignorance –Kevon Alacate Husband

Your free time is best occupied when it is used for self development- Kevon Alacate Husband

The only acceptable average is the one used in math. Other than such average shouldn't be your mindset- Kevon Alacate Husband

Success requires sacrifice - Kevon Alacate Husband

The true hallmark of a fool is that he speaks on things he has no knowledge or experience about. He believes his opinion is fact when in fact is it is his opinion. He is deceived by his opinion and his speech exposes him as a charlatan- Kevon Alacate Husband

Buying books is not an expense if you read them. It's an investment - Kevon Alacate Husband

We can't control the rain but we can walk with an umbrella. Preparation and planning is key- Kevon Alacate Husband

The mentality says it before the reality- Kevon Alacate Husband

All a man has in this life is a belief. Everything else is depends on such- Kevon Alacate Husband

You cannot do a dishonorable act in an honorable way- Kevon Alacate Husband

The problem with most people is they don't think or plan. Their life is a series of impulse decisions! - <u>Kevon Alacate Husband</u>

Rewards and consequences last longer than the actions which led to them. Choose wisely - <u>Kevon Alacate Husband</u>

If you think the impossible is impossible then it shall remain impossible. However if you think the impossible as possible you will achieve it. - <u>Kevon Alacate Husband</u>

Innovation is inspiration with a purpose- <u>Kevon Alacate Husband</u>

One man doing something is better than thousand men doing nothing and complaining- <u>Kevon Alacate Husband</u>

Low self esteem halts people from accepting and appreciating compliments-<u>Kevon Alacate Husband</u>

Just so you know your bad habits and vices cost you time and money-<u>Kevon Alacate Husband</u>

I don't care how long I've known you. If I realize you're a negative person and you have no intention of changing your thinking I will drop you faster than the people's elbow- <u>Kevon Alacate Husband</u>

Education might have a price tag but the most expensive cost a man can have is ignorance. That is expensive -Kevon Alacate Husband

I can teach you the formula but you still have to solve the equation by yourself - Kevon Alacate Husband

There are no ideal situations. Only half chances that positive thinkers turn into opportunities for success- Kevon Alacate Husband

A person who always waits on something to get started will have an excuse forever. It will be their reward- Kevon Alacate Husband

Knowledge and wisdom are the most paramount possessions a person can have. - Kevon Alacate Husband

You can't have success in 2018 when you're thinking like its 1998- Kevon Alacate Husband

What's the point in upgrading your phone, your car, your home but you wouldn't upgrade your thinking? - Kevon Alacate Husband

Being a non-participant in anything that concerns you is a sure way to confirm your mediocrity- Kevon Alacate Husband

What I don't know I will learn - Kevon Alacate Husband

Change is free but development is what comes at a cost but it is a worthy expenditure to have- Kevon Alacate Husband

If you think you can you will. Impossibility is just a self imposed limitation based on an inferior mindset- Kevon Alacate Husband

When desire meets knowledge and imagination it leads to creative innovation- Kevon Alacate Husband

A goal you're not working on is not a goal. That is called wishful thinking. Goals require time, energy, effort and sacrifice-Kevon Alacate Husband

It's ok to sleep and have dreams but it's never ok to sleep on your own dreams-Kevon Alacate Husband

If you do what everyone else is doing you will get what everyone else is getting -Kevon Alacate Husband

If you have a goal that you don't have to do anything special to accomplish it, you're still in your comfort zone-Kevon Alacate Husband

If you gave a negative thinker the most positive tools will he be successful? No... Because mindset trumps ability everytime-Kevon Alacate Husband

I will always accept constructive criticism, because you can't see the full picture when you're in the frame. - <u>Kevon Alacate Husband</u>

A negative mind will only see limitations. A positive mind will see opportunities to do the impossible- <u>Kevon Alacate Husband</u>

The best thing I have ever done in my life is to think positive.-<u>Kevon Alacate Husband</u>

If you only think about achieving what you deem realistic than you can't achieve the impossible. My goal is to make the impossible possible. Impossibility is a self imposed mindset- <u>Kevon Alacate Husband</u>

Basic economic principle and common sense will tell you don't buy what you cannot afford — <u>Kevon Alacate Husband</u>

ALACATE'S THOUGHTS AND EXPERIENCES

We have a society where men don't know how to be men. They run around having kids and not accepting the responsibilities. What we have here are just boys who grow up physically but not mentally. They are not men but they are grown boys. There are differences between being a man and a grown boy. Men handle their business, go to work, educate themselves, take care of their families/kids, develop character in their lives and in their offspring lives and thrive for self advancement. They cater for the needs of their children and don't seek credit for doing what they are supposed to. Grown Boys spend $300 dollars on sneakers while their kids drinking sugar water, sit on the block whole day drinking a 40, refuse to work and then get upset when they asked you for a dollar and you say no, chase every female, have multiple" baby mamas", and have no sort of desire for advancement of any kind. The reason society is messed up today is because it has more grown boys than men. Respect to all the men that do what they

are supposed to do and embrace their responsibilities.......
now with that said ...just let that sink in

Why would you hate on someone for trying to better
them self? I could never understand such. The fact that
someone is trying to do better with their respective life is
not a reason to dislike someone. You should be happy for
that person. The world has too much envy and jealousy
already. We are supposed to rejoice in each other's success
and achievements. Wouldn't you want your friends and
family to appreciate your desire to want a better life?
People acquire haters just because they made a positive
transition in life e.g. educational achievement, bought a
house, car, got married. If you dislike anyone because of
positive advancement in their respective life then you are
a hater and you need a mental overhaul in your thinking
and an attitude adjustment. ... now with that said ...just
let that sink in

Saying that you disagree, dislike or disapprove of
something is not the same as saying you hate something.
For example, I dislike baseball but I don't hate it. See
my point. People take words and associate their own
interpretation and meaning to it. If you do that you have
bad listening and communication skills. You should work
on that. ...now with that said just let that sink in

I have a question. What is the point of gossip? It serves no purpose. Most of the time 99% of what you hear in gossip is factually inaccurate. Why talk about someone or something you have no idea about? Spreading gossip only means that you allow yourself to be a vehicle for lies, half-truths deceit, and you embrace maliciousness. You are providing a medium for hurt and hatred to exist. Pretty much you have become a voice of unhealthy propaganda. A lot of people thrive on this and it gives meaning to their unfulfilled lives. So today, if someone comes to you with the latest gossip I advise you not to be a listening audience and allow yourself to be the next stop on the gossip train. Stop them there and don't promote or encourage their agenda....... now with that said. Just let that sink in

Sometimes we act like we never did anything to anybody. Like we have never hurt anyone. The truth is, no matter how nice of a person you are, just like you have been hurt in the past, you have also hurt someone in the past. Everyone has transgressed another person before. So moving forward never be too big to apologize even if it is something you can't remember. You don't have to remember because it didn't happen to you; it happened to them. Now with that said. Just let that sink in.

When you are tempted to complain remember this. While you are busy complaining someone else is out there hoping to be in your position. So today, stop complaining and start being appreciative of everything that you have. We spend too much time complaining and not much time in appreciation mode. Yes it can always be better but it can so easily always be worst….now with that said. Just let that sink in.

Do yourself a favor and call someone who you haven't spoken to in a while and just ask them if they are doing ok. Checking up on friends and family even if it is once in a while, helps to keep bonds and relationships intact. You never know what you might find out, who needs help or who can help you. Now with that said. Just let that sink in.

Everyone is looking for love from someone else but the reality is people need to learn how to love themselves first. How can you expect someone to love you and you don't even love yourself? Love yourself by setting standards, not allowing yourself to be disrespected and keeping in good company. People will only love you when you have unconditional love for yourself. Then they will know this person loves and accepts themselves, and if they love you they will have to meet your standards and give you respect as well…. now with that said. Just let that sink in.

I just wanted to talk on knowing when people are not good for you. Sometimes you have to let people go from your life not because they did something to you but because you are heading in a different direction from them. E.g if you are trying to obtain a masters degree you shouldn't be hanging out by the liquor store spending time with drunks. My point is, sometimes to get where you need to go you need to separate and isolate yourself from people who aren't conducive to your cause. People might react and say that you have changed or might make a dumb statement like "you ain't down for the homies or hood no more". Dont worry about that. Every successful person knows when to make a decision and when to separate "the goat from the sheep." Like minded people will always be found together so if you are on the pathway with others it will be a good indication of your intentions as a human being. Remember letting people out of your life doesn't mean that you are better than them but it means that you love yourself enough to know when people just aren't productive to your cause.... now with that said ...just let that sink in

Never think that you are too good or that you are above anything or anyone. A lot of people sometimes think that things are beneath their perceived "status". Just remember that just like everyone else when you were a baby someone else wipe your bottom and changed you when you were lying in your own excrement. My point being don't forget where you came from. Too many people believe that because they have a little more money or education than someone else that they are better than them. No one is better than anyone and your financial status/education doesn't make you better than anyone. Humility is an underrated concept. Some people fail to realize that no matter who you are, the time will come when you need someone else's help, so never be prideful. Being a narcissist never benefits you, as the saying goes "after pride comes a fall"..... now with that being said. Just let that sink in

Be careful of your accusations. Never call anyone a hypocrite because we have all made mistakes and no one is perfect. Question: Have you ever said you would not do something and you find yourself doing the exact same thing that you said you would never do? If you have done that (which unless you perfect then you haven't) then you pointing the finger back at yourself. Point being, don't focus on the mistakes that others make. Every circumstance is different and unique for every one. Worry about what is on your plate and not what someone else is eating. Try to focus on your mistakes and work on becoming a better person. Also, don't try to justify your own errors while expressing dislike for someone else's. Don't throw stones if you live in a glass house. If you have to use the term hypocrite make sure you are perfect and have no flaws..... now with that said ...just let that sink in

Stop listening to other people's opinion of you. Start rejecting all the negative stereotypes. Don't allow anybody to tell you who you are and what your value is. A lot of times people tell you stuff because they can't accomplish what you have accomplished. They gave up on themselves and they want you to give up on yourself. So reject their no's, shouldn't, can'ts and impossible's. Personally, a lot of people have told me I shouldn't even be alive I should just curl up and die....You don't see me shopping for coffins, do you? Ignore negative point of views and affirmations about you. Point being start embracing yourself and appreciate who you are. A lot of people delight in seeing failures and if you are one of those people you are a hater and in need of a mental overhaul.........now with that said just let that sink in

You always have to be loyal to yourself. Stop trying to prove loyalty to other people when you are not even loyal to yourself. Too many people misinterpret loyalty for something else. They often confuse loyalty as "being down with the group". Be loyal to your own goals, dreams, aspirations and personal development. You must recognize that you need to seek after your interest and like William Shakespeare said "To thine own self be true". Be true in your everyday motives and beliefs. Don't compromise who you are (morals, beliefs, values) for anyone. Be faithful to your cause. At the end of your it's a" one to a box theory". Unfortunately, a lot of young people confuse loyalty with stupidity and end up incarcerated doing 10-15 years just for being "loyal", So today I urge you to show a strong feeling of support or allegiance to yourself. Be loyal to yourself. If you are going to be loyal to someone else but not yourself you're in a bad head space..... now with that said ...Just let that sink in

Let's do this. Question ? 7+3=10, 6+4=10,8+2=10. Not because someone does things different from you, makes your way right and their way wrong. …. now with that said ...just let that sink in

Take care of yourself. Learn to refresh your body, mind and soul. Take time off to give yourself a little breathing room. Too many people don't take time to smell the roses or give themselves a bit of rest and relaxation. Don't get caught up in the rat race of life. I encourage you to spend time with friends and family. Have a laugh and lighten the load on your shoulders. Too many people are busy "chasing that money" and have nothing to show for it. How about playing with your kids ever so often or volunteering for a cause or even checking up on loved ones. Life isn't about how much money you make but it is more about how much memories you create. Today take some time and appreciate the simple pleasures of life. You never know how long they will be here for or how long you will be here for………… now with that said ...just let that sink in

Ok people lets do this. When I go outside and hear the level of conversation which comes out the mouth of our nations youth I wonder where did we go wrong. A lot of these kids out there cussing up a storm in public like its nobody's business. I wonder what happens at home? Sometimes I feel like society is getting dumber and dumber everyday. It is time someone tells these kids to expand their vocabulary and increase their knowledge. How are you going to get a job if every 3 words that come out your mouth is f-bomb or some sort of profanity. Parents you are responsible for your kids until they are adults. Teach them about representing themselves in the proper manner. Inform them about Civility in a conversation. Respect, manners and etiquette are attributes that are never overrated and always appreciated. Unless of course the parents don't have these qualities then the "machines left the factory broken" then you can't fix them. Finally parents, be careful of the quality of product you produce at home. Remember when you done with raising your children the rest of society has to deal with them.... and society will not love or care for them like you do........Now good people with that said ..... just let that sink in

Let's talk about people who always misinterpreting everything that you say and turn it into an argument. I say don't have conversations with those people. These people apparently have one track mind and are incapable of having regular conversations. They want to tell you what you mean and what you are saying. I have a quote which I came up with for situations like these..."When people misinterpret what you are trying to say it is good communication principle to try to clarify yourself.... however, when people are committed to misinterpreting what you saying and they are claimung that you are saying something you are not, never try to explain yourself to them. Fools never like correction and are deceived by the errors of their ways and thinking"- Alacate) . ... I hope this helps you in your daily dialogue and interaction with people .... if you are one of those people who get offended for every little thing with everybody you have a mental communication problem, the whole world isn't out to offend you .... now with that said ...just let that sink in

Parents you have to set a better example. It doesn't matter who you are, your children will look at your life as an example. Show your children and teach them the right characteristics and qualities to be a success in society. Don't show them your life as an example of what not to do but show them your life as an example of what to do. Your life is the greatest living testimony in your children's life. Whether you like it or not, they learn from what they see not what you say. Don't set an example of compromise. because the kids will eventually compromise other aspects of their lives when they get older. Pretty much I am saying they won't take you seriously or anything else seriously (E.g their health, the laws, their principles.)You are sending them down the highway of compromise. The old adage of "do as I say and not as I do" is an outdated and irresponsible concept and a pathetic excuse for any adult/ parent/ guardian to make. If you are making that excuse you have failed not only yourself but your children, Be the example you want your kids to follow....... now with that said ...just let that sink in

You need to stop doubting yourself. That needs to stop today. You need to get out of the mindset of negativity. I have a question. Would you just punch, damage and hurt yourself physically? If the answer is no then why would you do it to yourself mentally. Even before a word is said a lot of people just mentally assault themselves with negativity. Its one thing when people try to kill your dreams but it is another thing when you attack your own dreams/ goals and aspirations. That is not cool. When you have ideas in your head even before it comes out you just obliterate it for no reason. Start embracing your ideas. Think positive. How can you live and accomplish the dream if you refuse to let it out of your head? Today I charge you to start thinking about the possibilities and embrace your ideas. Change your mindset and develop your mind into a concept of positive thinking. By killing your own dreams before you start working on them you are not only denying yourself but you are denying the world of your idea.....The only failed idea is the one you never worked on...... Don't let negativity kill your dreams...... now with that said ...just let that sink in

Not everyone is trying to outsmart you. Not everyone with a different point of view is stupid. Not everyone messing with your intelligence. .. sometimes you have to take people at their word.... stop trying to read between the lines when there isn't anything to read. That's the problem with a lot of people. A lot of people overthink and by doing that sometimes they create problems that were non-existent. They are going to lose alot of relationships and friendships because of their own prejudices, judgements and misinterpretations without basis. ..change your mindset..now with that said just let that sink in

Stop looking at what others have and envying them. You don't know what they did to get it. We need to get out of the mentality of looking at the grass on the other side of the fence, focus on your own grass. People are becoming envious, jealous and filled with malice because someone acquired or gained something or some achievement. Focus on you. Don't worry about others acquisitions when you are not trying to improve yourself. Develop yourself. A lot of times we tend to see what others have but we don't see their struggles too, but we are quick to judge. We should bypass the stage of trying to "keep up with the Joneses" I hope this helps someone struggling with jealously or envy.......... now with that said ...just let that sink in

Never and I repeat never allow someone to control your life. Don't give them that authority to tell you what you have to be and what you can't be. This is your life and at the end of the day only you are responsible for the decisions you make. Don't let people dictate your life. It is one thing when someone encourages you and promotes a positive agenda with regards to your development but it is a totally different scenario when they try to control your existence. Telling you who to date, what clothes to wear, what career to pursue and where to go etc.... if you have someone in your life that is trying to control your movements or your daily activities you need to remove that person and lessen their influence on your life. This is your life to live. That person who is trying to control your life, maybe you should ask them why don't they do what they are telling you to do with your life, with their respective life.......... now with that said ...just let that sink in

Its time you young men realize that there is absolutely no point in embracing the gangster/ badman lifestyle. That choice of lifestyle only leads to a quicker than expected arrival to the following places... grave, jail and hospital. There is no future in dealing up in that kind of life. Being a gangster is not cool, there is no glamour in it. Unless you have a liking for the police to be constantly harassing you and your family or you have a burning desire for bullets to pierce you skin and vital organs, why would you want to associate yourself with such negativity. On top of that by being involved in a gang not only puts you in danger but also endangers your family and loved ones. You are not a man if you are willing to put your family in danger course. It is a shame that more young men have embraced that type of living rather than pursue educational and goal oriented pursuits. It is sad that they rather bang for the block/hood and they don't even own a piece of property in the neighborhood.......... now with that said ...just let that sink in

If you are constantly negative don't expect people not to feel that energy. Negativity comes in many different forms. ....unbelief in one's self, always looking at the cons of a situation, discouraging others in their pursuit of goals and ideas, mentally putting down yourself, being a hater... etc... sooner or later those around you will realize that you exude negativity and will not want to be closely associated with you because of your mindset. Today I urge you to develop your mindset to divulge and delight yourself in positive thoughts, patterns and scenarios. Nothing will get better for you by thinking negative, so why would you do it? Your mind is the single most powerful tool you have in your arsenal of intelligence. Don't use it to be counterproductive. I don't think God would appreciate you misusing that gift......now with that said ...just let that sink in

No matter what decision you make in life you always have to deal with the outcome. Whether it be good or bad it is a decision you have to live with. Too many times people don't think things through and end up in a state of remorse or hardship. Too many young women have babies with "grown boys" because they got "swag" but with that swag often comes no ambition. Too many young men join gangs and want to pull that trigger not realizing that they giving themselves life sentences. Too many people get behind the wheel of a car intoxicated and cause injury or death to themselves or someone else...... the point I am making here is that we need to think things through as individuals. See the long term consequences and rewards. Carefully consider your options because when that decision is made you have to live with it for the rest of your days and it may also affect others in your vicinity..................now people.... now with that said ...just let that sink in

Let me encourage everyone to be grateful. Life is precious and in-spite of what situations you may have going on, always be grateful. Appreciate the fact that you are in the land of the living. Some people went to sleep last night and never woke up : they didn't get a chance to say i love you to their loved one's. You have that opportunity. Today you are alive, embrace the idea and develop a attitude of appreciation for the little things in life. Your creator has allowed you to continue to exist and your life is referred to in the present tense. You should acknowledge and be grateful to him for that............. now with that said ...just let that sink in

It is time we stop associating alcohol and drugs to a good time. Neither is necessary to have a good time. The illusion of those substances is to make you feel good and have you believe you are having a good time. What is good about you being so drunk that you're left lying down incoherent in the middle of the street, you so high you start seeing things and attack loved ones or having no control over your bodily movement because you are high or intoxicated? What is thrilling or exhilarating about that? How many deaths does drunk driving cause a year or how many families have been affected by alcoholism and drug use daily? Now I know that some of these examples are worst case scenarios but they are all realistic and possible. (See Murphy's Law). In all the situations mentioned the one constant variable is drugs/alcohol. If you need either one to have a good time then something is missing from your life and I guarantee you that you won't find the solution in that....... now with that said just let that sink in

Be careful of what message you are communicating to people. There is a difference between what you say/do/ how you represent yourself and how it is interpreted. This is different from caring what people say and think about you. Your reputation is one of the most important things you have in life and you should try your best to maintain it. Combine creditable Reputation with good character and you should be unstoppable. Too many people have a don't care mentality about the image they are presenting and they end up misrepresenting themselves. They may be well educated but because of the "marketing of themselves" they can be viewed as idiots. You have to sell yourself as you would sell a product. The one thing that can hurt you long term is when you miscommunicate your ideas, intentions and standards. A lot of people are denied job/educational/developmental opportunities simply based on their lack of proper representation of themselves. Do yourself a favor and represent yourself in an esteemed and respectable manner so as to give yourself credibility and respectability. You never know who is watching and what opportunities await you. Don't discredit yourself............ now with that said just let that sink in

I wish to engage your thought processes on the topic .... fight videos. Our young men and women seem for no reason to be uncontrollably angry and eager to record it. Too many people gain a sense of pride from fighting and posting it online. Young people please know that these videos never disappear and even if you have changed your life in 5-10 years the video will still be in circulation. Many young people today will be denied opportunities because of such (educational, job/career opportunities). Just for the record it is not cool. The decisions you make will affect your future regardless of who you are. Why not find a more constructive avenue to use your apparent love of videos. Making a vine video, funny skit or something worthwhile to benefit you or your community. Try to ascend to that higher level of thinking. Use your free time to develop your skill. The next video which is recorded of you can be your calling card for life ....how will you be remembered and recognized in the future? .... Now with that said just let that sink in

I am swinging for the fences and people will be "pulling up their socks" after reading this. Just because someone else is born in another country doesn't give you a right to harass, intimidate and harm them. I don't normally use this type of rhetoric but it is time this ignorant level of thinking stop. No one and I repeat no one is better than anyone else simply because of the cover on their respective passport and if you think you are better due to your place of birth then you are severely mistaken Some of you may know I am of West Indian heritage and in the year 2009 I was working at a call center and I had a person indicated to me that me and my kind (specifically my mother) should go back where we came from. This person indicated a dislike for immigrants and in particular West Indians. Of course the company's management tried to sweep it under the rug instead of combating the issue. I have forgiven the company and the person. This dilemma happens every day to millions of workers. These types of people are a cancer to any organization. The belief and thinking of these types of people is at the bottom of the abyss of emotional intelligence. I want to remind people that the nationality of your passport does not make you any better or worse off than anyone else. All it does is make you unique and special and simply states the geographical location of your birth and you should be proud of that............ now with that said ...just let that sink in

Just a reminder to keep a positive mindset. Continue working hard and expect results. Don't be easily discouraged. Something I started doing is that every day in front of my mirror I reaffirm my goals, dreams and aspirations to myself. That helps me to overcome the past hardships of the previous day. I refocus and re-channel my energies to ensure that before I leave my home that my mindset is positive. Of course with life you will have setbacks but it is your reaction to those setbacks that is what determines how you move forward. I want to encourage everyone today who is reading this to keep your mind mentally healthy with good vibes, daily affirmations and the belief that you will accomplish your dreams. This is something Ipracticeeveryday. Regardless of who will discourage you or encourage you, only you can determine your frame of mind..... now with that said ...just let that sink in

I want to speak to the mature folks. Be careful of how you treat the younger generation. Watch the words you say to them and how you interact with them. Parents, teachers/ Principals, grandparents, elder siblings, Sunday school teachers etc. all have a meaningful impact on the younger generation. Teachers/ Principals in particular I am holding most accountable today. Unfortunately, too many times I hear of young people saying that they have been called names like stupid, dummy; idiot and even being told they will never amount to anything by the supposed educators of society. I myself have been told condescending words from teachers before and I was supposed to be a "nuisance to society" (by the way I turned out to be my high school valedictorian). Shame on those in the education system that resort to verbal/mental/emotional condemnation to the youths. You are supposed to educate the youths, elevate their thinking and feed them the fire of inspiration. Inspire the next generation of greatness. Respect to all the teachers who develop young minds into tomorrow's world beaters. Luckily for me I had one of those. The impact and potential those in the education system will have on our nation's youth is unmatched in potential by any other sector. If you are an educator in a public or private school system I am sure that your job description is not to discourage the student you are receiving a salary to teach… if you discourage students you sir/ma'am are an unfit teacher and I make no apologies for saying such…. now with that said …just let that sink in

Overcoming your environment. Your environment doesn't determine who you are. Your ambition does, your drive does, and your goal does. Not because you were born in the Hood/Ghetto means that you have to be a product of your environment. Too many people walk around sounding silly making statements like "I'm hood for life" or "I'm straight up ghetto" and so on. Why would anyone want to live that way for life? Elevate your mind so that you can have the intelligence to know that while you may have been born in the "ghetto" it is not a final destination or resting place for you in life. You should always want better for yourself and your family. How about working on talents, concentrating on your education, developing ideas and products which can help you to gain the required level on financial stability so that the "ghetto life" is past tense for you? Don't worry about the people who might say you "trying to get uppity on us now". Forget them. They aren't necessary to your life and your cause. Everyone has a duty to socially and mentally uplift themselves. If they don't want to then that's their problem, not yours. If people don't like you because you "moving on up" then they never liked you. You being born in the ghetto isn't your fault but if you spend your entire life there, then that's on you.........now with that said .....Just let that sink in

I wish to speak on volunteering information. Not everybody has a right to the details of your private life. As a rule of thumb you shouldn't just go about volunteering information especially to people you are not close with. Friends, acquaintances and co-workers don't need to know everything that goes on in your life. When you constantly volunteer information you allow people to gain access to details that would otherwise remain confidential. Now in the event that you have a quarrel /disagreement or fallout with that person, if they are angry or have a malicious spirit they may choose to reveal information on you especially on social media. Just as a rule of thumb, don't tell anyone your personal detail regardless of how cool you think you are with that individual. Privacy is something everyone should maintain in their lives and when you tell someone your personal details they might not regard your privacy like you will theirs. Posting private information on social media is not wise as there are too many green snakes in the green grass. Remember if you don't tell anyone your personal details they won't have a chance to use it against you...........now with that said just let that sink in...

Unless a man is disabled, laid off, injured or has a terminal illness there is no reason for him to stay at home. Real men understand the need to be employed and take care of their household. ..... And also no woman should ever be supporting a healthy full grown man. No self respecting female should be with a man who refuses to contribute to the house.... now with that said just let that sink in

I don't normally talk on relationships but I will make an exception....To all the insecure men and women out there, here is a piece of advice.... Your significant other will leave you not because of someone else but because of your insecurity. You are creating problems in your relationship because of your insecurity. The more insecure you are the higher the chances of you losing the person. Nobody wants to deal with insecurities. When you are threatened by no one and you're feeling threatened that is when you start being controlling. If you start questioning or being jealous every friend of the opposite sex your partner has it won't be too long before you start being the abusive, controlling type person. You are your relationship and your own biggest enemy......... now with that said just let that sink in

Let's talk about dealing with haters. Rule one: pay them no mind. In life no matter what you do you will always have people who will hate on you, gossip on you and those who will never like you. Never ever let them get inside of your head. I have a policy and I believe it will work for you - Don't and I repeat don't waste time to respond, react or engage in any sort of communication what them. When you ignore it shows that you have the power to mentally psych them out so that they cannot get to you. Once you can mentally evade them you have already won this battle, just continue to work on yourself. If someone doesn't like you that is not your business, that's their problem. Never pay any attention to haters; they are already paying attention to you. Keep your head up and focus on your immediate goals…. Remember only if you let them get to you they will exist…………… now with that said just let that sink in

Letting go of anger and hate. I should start by saying there is nothing wrong in being angry. Anger is a very fundamental human emotion. However, when one's anger is allowed to go unchecked for a long period of time it leads to resentment, bitterness, emotional discord, mental uneasiness and the end result is hate. When you hate your emotions are off balance and you will not be able to focus and have a normal life. You will always worry about getting back at someone for something they did or you will always see things in a negative light. Your anger will only lead you down a road which will result in you being deeply hurt. Learn to forgive and move on. Having hatred is like throwing away the oven because you got burnt once. You have more to lose by allowing hate to become your primary emotion. Stop living with hate…. You are only hurting yourself and God forbid that you might end up hurting someone you really care for……. now with that said just let that sink in

Let's talk about love. I don't know what the question is, but I know that love is my answer. The world is messed up today because a lot of people didn't received love at the appropriate time. Everyone is looking for love. The problem is that people look for it in the wrong places…… gangs, drugs, one night stands, bad friendships etc. Point is that God is love. You love God then you can love yourself and then you can properly love everyone. Love can solve most of the world's issues. Parents/guardians encouraging and giving your children the right type of love can help the society in avoiding a lot of the issues today. Our jails and cemeteries are filled with people who were looking for love and never got it. Love must start at home. Love is the most powerful tool in the world. Some simple gestures of love include greetings, kind words, respectful compliments, fist bumps, handshakes, hugs etc… I encourage all to show love to someone. Love is the way forward. Remember love is the answer……….. Now with that said just let that sink in

One day while driving to work one of my favorite songs came on my iPod - Bob Marley's "is this love". A particular part of the song goes "I want to love you and treat you right". I thought maybe I should talk about this. Bob makes a lot of sense here because if you do love someone

49

you would want to treat them right. If you have love in your heart you would want to treat everybody right. Your friends, relatives, kids, neighbors, people on the street, co-workers, customers etc.... Love doesn't require you to be obsessed with a particular individual but it does require you to want to give everyone their due respect. If you say you love someone your actions will show it. You will most definitely treat them right. It will be so natural to you. Anyway people, let the love continue.............. now just let that sink in.

When the meteorologist says "there is going to be a 20% chance of rain" mentally I hear "there is going to be 80% chance of sunshine." Train your mind to see the positive in every situation and stop focusing on the negative..... Now with that said just let that sink in

I want to encourage those who are reading this today who might be struggling to make progress, to continue to hold on. Don't look at someone else who has accomplished something that you may be trying to accomplish and become frustrated. Different people succeed at different paces and ages. Some people become successful at 25 and for others it might be 45. Point is, continue to work on your craft. You have to continue to believe that your hard work will pay off. Don't worry about what others have accomplished, worry about your goals. Too many people are discouraged when they aren't making progress. All this time you should have continued to keep the belief that you will be successful. Sometimes you have to be unsuccessful 100 times and then on the 101st attempt you might finally succeed. There might be someone reading this whom I know nothing about, however I do believe you will be successful; If I don't know you and believe you can be successful, why won't you believe?....... now with that said just let that sink in

Passing the blame. This is the common practice in society and it is a plague in my opinion. It happens everywhere, churches, workplaces, between siblings/ family members, friends, professional sports. It seems like no one wants to accept responsibility. Everyone just keeps passing the buck. Hardly ever does anyone say "I accept full responsibility." Too many people cower to duck responsibilities. This scenario is most sad when parents neglect their children and try to blame someone else for their misfortune. Just so we understand your children are your responsibility, no one else's. When mothers and fathers shun their duties to their children, the fabric of society is stained and we cannot expect the next generation to uplift themselves or even assume responsibility for anything...thus the passing of the buck continues.......now just let that sink in

I want to talk about limitations. First rule, don't have them. Never limit your mind as to what you have the ability to do and not to do. Try thinking outside of the box. Not to sound cliché but once you put your mind to it you can accomplish anything that you want. When you limit you self you are mentally saying to yourself "I don't have it in me." However, as the story with the choo-choo goes "I think I can, I think I can" should be your mentality. When you go after the impossible you energize yourself and your body/spirit/mind will be committed to accomplishing the goal; you can then push through the physical/mental/emotional barriers. Every desire you have start from inside and go through a psychological process. Limitations are what you set for yourself. Today I want you to charge your inner being, do not set limitations but set goals. After you've accomplished those goals, set new and higher goals. The only limit you should have is no limitations.............now people just let that sink in

It's that time of the year when everyone is looking for the next year. On top of that everyone is busy making New Year resolutions. I have a habit of not getting into the practice of such because dates do not correspond with the ability to change one's behavior. Change comes along when one is convinced enough that it is necessary. Calendar dates are irrelevant. The desire for better can come at any time. However, there are those who would still insist on having New Year resolutions; to this I will say if you are waiting on Dec. 31st/Jan1st to start making positive changes in your life you have already lost ground

because your changes are not going "cold turkey". You probably should have started a long time ago to enable that date to have credibility. Some groundwork should have been laid down for the foundation of your pursuit towards positive changes, thus making the transition easier.......
Now just let that sink in

My words shall be about seeing the positive in every situation. Too many times we train our minds to look at things and even people in a condescending view. Example: you might see a homeless person hustling or begging for money and one might say they need to get a job or look how dirty he is. Instead of using that negative approach, focus your thinking on the positive for example: at least he isn't robbing anyone! I remember when my grandmother passed away that was the most horrible time in my life by any stretch. I knew that I'm always talking about positivity and always encouraging but this time I was really tested. After a good long cry, I started reflecting on all the good times and fun moments we had, all the great cooking, all the times she saved me from getting spanked and my whole attitude began to change. When it was time for the funeral I considered it an honor to carry my grandmother casket. While the atmosphere was sad I kept positive in the fact at least I was there to help carry her casket. Before the casket closed I kissed her on the face and I knew that I was the last person to touch her before she was buried. I take a lot of solace from that as well as from the fact that my cousin used one of my quotes in the eulogy. Death which was supposed to be an entirely negative/depressive situation came out as a positive/uplifting for me, because of my mindset. I encourage everyone today to see and embrace the opportunity to be positive in even the most disheartening of situations............Now just let that sink in

I want to talk to about making excuses. It seems today that everyone has an excuse and it has become a trend amongst us. We have become a society which relies on our "reasons not to" than "reasons to". Common sayings like "Do I really need a GED" or "When the kids are older maybe I will go back to college", "I'm too fat to exercise", "I am going to start once I can find the time" ..Etc... today I want to encourage you to train your mind from being a "going to/want to doer" to an "accomplisher". Stop finding reasons not to do and start finding reasons to do. Wishful thinking is only nice when one follows and accomplishes the task they wish upon. Get into the habit of following through on things that you wish to do. So today I encourage you to get up off the couch and start making steps towards moving forward in life. Start filling out that college application; enroll in the GED classes that you have been procrastinating with for the last 8 months. Go down to the DMV and get your ID/learners permit, apply for that promotion that you saw advertised on the notice board at your job. My point is get up and get going. Your words and intentions are just hot air and thoughts unless you do something about it…..now with that said people …just let that sink in.

If you are waiting on things to be secure then you're not acting on faith. Faith is when you step out on a belief with no tangible means or visible evidence of a chance to be successful. If you always waiting on this or that you aren't acting on faith, you're acting on evidence- Alacate. Inspiration from Hebrews 11.1

Good people….I want to create a fictional scenario for you inspired by a man I think is the greatest motivational speaker of all time Zig Ziglar. What if one day you were home and I walked into your living room and started throwing garbage all over your living room what would you do? Probably stop me, whip me, point a gun at me and make me clean it up, call the police …. Point being you would not allow me to enter your house and desecrate it without me facing some sort of consequence. The garbage in the living room can be cleaned up but what about the garbage you allow to take up space in your mind. No one can clean that up but you. Stop allowing people to fill up your mind with garbage. If anyone is discouraging you and dumping negativity, condescending words and action, doubt, distrust, and despair in your mind you need to stop them immediately. Don't allow anyone such a privilege. After they have finished offloading their "mental trash" in your mind you are the one stuck with the task of cleaning it up. Therefore, I suggest the same way you wouldn't allow anyone to trash your living room, don't allow anyone to do that to your mind... Guard you mind..........now just let that sink in

If you are reading this you should be grateful that you are alive. You made it through the year. So many people didn't make it. So give thanks and praises to your creator for protecting you. It could have so easily been different... everyday things happen, car accidents, shooting (both accidental and intentional), construction accidents, heart attacks/strokes etc. All these could have taken your life but God decided that you will live another day, and then another and then another...., I remember that my grandmother was 95 years old and I was telling myself that I will go to see her for her 100th birthday but that was not to be. It was not given that she would live to be 100 and it is not given for everyone, tomorrow is not promised. So I want to encourage all to be grateful, not just because you made it through the year, but be grateful every day. Never take life for granted............now just let that sink in

Let's talk about avoiding the negative. You are into a New Year and while I don't believe in New Year resolutions I do believe in improving oneself on a regular consistent basis. In order to do this, one of the things we must do is avoid negativity in all its forms. Negative people, activities, lifestyles, choices, situations, TV shows, books etc … must all be deleted. Chances are, if you don't remove yourself from negative things they will have a negative effect on you. Instead start embracing positive lifestyle activities. Spend your time engrossed in positivity: watch uplifting TV programs, read books that enhance self-esteem, spend more time around the people that encourage and believe in you. Write down a list of positive attributes you have no matter how small they are and everyday set a goal to develop one or more uplifting traits about yourself. If you do that every day for one year you would have developed 365 positive helpful traits to add to what you already have. Pretty much you would have inspired and re-invented yourself at least 365 times over. ……………now with that said just let that sink in

I have a simple exercise for you. If you have an area near you which has an echo point, I want you to shout out the following words "Positivity and Love". After that shout out "Negativity and Hate"... Notice for both, you hear the echo. Point being, whatever you speak out your mouth is what will come back to you. If you speak and practice positive things your return will be positive but if your speech and mindset is negative the results will be negative. What you give out is what you will get back.......Now with that said just let that sink in

Let me take you back to the 1800's and tell you about an experiment carried out by French Entomologist Jean-Henri Fabre. He took some Processionary caterpillars (known to follow each other blindly) and assembled several of them in a circle with each one touching the other (front to rear, rear to front) around the rim of a flower pot. In the center of the flower pot he inserted pine needles: a favorite food of the caterpillars. The caterpillars simply followed each other in a circle for 7days blindly until they fell of the flower pot and died of starvation/exhaustion with food less than 6 inches away. The Point being stop being a follower and learn to take control of your destiny. Don't be afraid to break rank with friends and pursue what you know is your calling. Sometimes not fitting in might just be the best thing you have ever done........now with that said just let that sink in

Let's talk about mediocrity. People tend to accept their status quo and hence fail to make progress in an effective way. People will accept living just to get by and pass on that lifestyle to their kids and it becomes the order of the day. If you're doing everything the same way every day but hoping for a lucky break join the line of people trying to pseudo-succeed. However, if you work hard on accomplishing task extraordinarily daily, your desire to leave mediocrity behind will be greater. Warren Bennis, a leadership studies professor in the University of South California was quoted as saying: "Excellence is a better teacher than mediocrity". You can always do better. Try reaching your full potential by setting goals and actively pursuing them. Are you satisfied with just getting by? Are you happy with just paying your bills and having little or no money left over to pursue things that you like? Is your life enhanced by just meeting the minimum standard required? If not, I believe you just discovered and obtained the first step to overcoming this - Realization. Now you have some work to do, release your mindset from the chains of mediocrity…. now with that said just let that sink in

Interesting scenario. It snowed today and I'm not really fond of it, but yet then I got up and left the house and went about my daily proceedings. While walking in the snow I realized I was walking in the footsteps of others and the path was no good for me. So I decided to make my own pathway in the snow and I was able to get to my destination quicker than the common trodden path. My Point being, sometimes you have to be a leader and not a follower. Blaze your own trail and don't be afraid to make your own way. It may be different to others but you should always try to be an innovator and not an imitator. The reward may be greater than you know ….now with that said just let that sink in

I was reading the oh so familiar biblical story of David and Goliath. Upon researching some scientific facts it was estimated that Goliath was predicted to be between 6 feet 9 inches and 9 feet tall (depending on the various listed measurement at the time) and roughly over 300 pounds and in prime shape (a superb physical and intimidating specimen). David couldn't be no more than 5 feet tall at the time but yet still David had the confidence and the faith in God that this giant of a man could be defeated. Why? Because David had belief in his ability and faith in God Almighty. We all know how that story went with David conquering the giant and changing the course of history for his people. Today I want to remind you that regardless of the obstacles standing in your way, it can be conquered. Faith in God and believing in your ability are quintessential to you overcoming challenges in your life. Walk with the belief that you can obtain success regardless of situations, setbacks, challenges, naysayers and so-called impossible task. If God almighty is who you trust in and sincerely believe, you can turn impossible into possible… now with that said just let that sink in.

Let me start this affirmation by telling you about an animal: the flea. While it is considered a pest, the flea is quite an extraordinary specimen of nature due to its small size. However, it has the ability to jump hundreds of times its own height. That would be the human equivalent of jumping the empire state building. In flea circuses, they are trained by placing them in a jar with a covered lid and each time the flea jumps it hits the lid of the jar. Eventually, the flea starts jumping to the height of the jar because it has been conditioned to do so even when the lid of the jar is off. My point being, don't let people put limitations on you. Unlike the flea you have a say in producing your maximum effort every time. People limitations of you are not your limitations so don't abide by their limits. That is not your concern. Never allow anyone to put a limit on you. They can only do that if you allow them to……….. now with that said just let that sink in.

Here is an interesting scenario. I was trying to catch the elevator in the building and there was a gentleman who held the door opened for me and I was grateful and thanked him. He in turn responded with pleasantries and what happened for the next 30 seconds changed both our days. He asked me how was my day going and I told him great. I responded by saying that I always have good days; I decided that a long time ago. He asked when exactly, I said when I was born I decided that. We laughed and I told him "I have never had a bad day in my life just bad things happen on good days. If you have a bad day then just try missing one of them". He responded as I was getting off the elevator. "With that personality/attitude I know you're going to have a great day". You never know who you are interacting with therefore it's important to pass along positivity. That gentleman may have been having a rough day but by me being positive and embracing a healthy / joyful perception of life may have just changed the course of his day. It's not all rainbows and butterflies in my life but I see the positive and develop a spirit of appreciation. ....now carry on and be cheerful...... now with that said just let that sink in

A topic I wish to speak on is dealing with the death of a loved one. As you know most of my post are about inspiration and positive living so one may ask what is positive about someone's passing? Let me start by saying that death is a part of the life process. A time to be born and a time to die. It is all part of the circle of life. Nothing can compare to losing someone you love but even then you can find positives to dwell on. Think about the deceased love for you. Think about the good times you had with them. Think about the lessons taught. A useful resource which helps is the bible. It gives lots of helpful scriptures when enduring the loss of a loved one e.g. Psalms 147 verse 3: *He heals the brokenhearted and binds up their wounds,* John 16 verse 22: *So also you have sorrow now, but I will see you again, and your hearts will rejoice, and no one will take your joy from you.* Revelations 21.verse 4: *He will wipe away every tear from their eyes, and death shall be no more, neither shall there be mourning, nor crying, nor pain anymore, for the former things have passed away.* There are many more scriptures which you can find to help you in your time of great loss. One of the things I noticed about a loved one's passing is that we tend to appreciate the things we normally take for granted ….. Three most important things are God, Family and life. Death tends to bring things into prospective for us…. I dedicate this to all of you who have lost someone that you dearly loved. God heal your soul at this time

I will not mix my words with sugar, spice and everything nice. It is time women stop pulling down each other. Too much jealously exists among women for the most trivial of things. Women hating each other because of a dress or a pair of shoes, because your friend got a new boyfriend, because someone got married etc…. Just so you know that is not cool. Women face obstacles every day that men are sometimes oblivious about so the last thing women need to do is be in mortal combat mode against each other. So what if the other woman got married or has on a prettier dress than you? Is that a reason to hate her? Some people tend to say well once women are together you will have some sort of issue but I disagree. If you have mature positive thinking women together they can co-exist. You would think women should be united and look out for each other. If you hate another women because of a positive acquisition or lifestyle change guess what…. you're a hater and that is a really an unattractive trait. That is one of the reasons why a lot of men don't respect women because some don't even have respect for each other ....now with that said just let that sink in

I would like to engage your mind in this topic: **Family**. Let me say firstly that family is the most quintessential institution in society. A lot depends on family. This is where most people will gain their moral compass for a lifetime and so where any nation's potential future can be formed. Family bonds have been required for centuries and were key to survival and development of mankind. In today's world a lot of society problems originate because of family issues. Too many families have infighting and relatives can go sometimes years without communication due to disputes many of which are petty (while some can be legitimate). Dr Herb True (a professor at the university of Notre Dame) suggests an exercise which I strongly endorse. Every 2-3 months close your eyes and imagine that all your family members were totally and suddenly dead (no warning). I ask you is, it worth it? It doesn't matter whose fault it was, the important thing is that we all at least try an attempt at reconciliation. Stop letting tangibles such as money, a spouse, property etc... alienate you from family. At the end of the day family is all you have and the rest of world they will not value you as your family would................ Now with that said just let that sink in

I want to take a different turn in my topic and address a certain group of people. If you are one of those people who are arguing with everybody under the sun then you are my target audience today. Let me start by saying that while I recognize that nobody is perfect you need to stop picking arguments and recognize sometimes the problem is with you. Watch the way you interact with others. Your tone, your face, your facial expressions, your aggressive attitude etc…. Everybody on the planet is not wrong. The harsh truth is that you are. When you have that type of attitude sooner or later you will destroy personal and professional relationships. If everywhere you have constant falling outs and disagreements with others remember that you are the one constant variable in that situation. You are probably the type to say "Well I don't need anybody" once again you are wrong. The garbage man needs the doctor when he is sick and the doctor needs the garbage men or else he would be living in a waste disposal.(No man is an island) Point being, if you continue with this behavior you will end up alone in this world and develop emotional dissatisfaction. If you're the type who is in constant quarrel with father/ mother/sibling/aunty/uncle/co-workers/social media etc take some time and do a little introspection. Sometimes the problem is within us and we need to recognize that and make the change ……………….. Now with that said just let that sink in

I am going to talk about standing up for what you believe in. First off, never allow peer pressure to get to you regardless of who or what is offered in exchange. There is no reward which can be greater than maintaining and keeping a moral /personal/spiritual standard you set for yourself. Let me give you a story which happened to me in my teenage years. I used to take Saturday lessons and after class I went and hung out with a "friend". I was probably 15 years old at the time and my friend went into the store and bought a coca cola and to my surprise some cigarettes. I only had money for transport that day and it was a really hot day. I asked him for some of the cola. He made me a proposition that if I took a puff of the cigarette I could have some cola. Guess what: up to this day I don't know what that cola tasted like. I was not about to comprise my beliefs and my standards for Coca cola. I was able to keep my beliefs intact and I am proud to say that I don't smoke and a strict teetotaler (I don't drink alcohol). That day I made a decision which altered my life in the most positive way. If I took that cigarette that day chances are I may have developed an addiction to nicotine and I might have been a smoker for about 15 plus years. I want to encourage both young and old individuals to always make the right decision. NEVER, EVER, EVER allow anyone to pressure you into making a decision which you know is not right …………. Now with that said just let that sink in

This topic is on Spending and Saving. First off, let me start by saying everyone owes it to them self to be financially

responsible. There are a lot of lessons to be learned in the area of finances. Stop spending money on things you don't need. The principle of basic economics is based on scarcity i.e. you only have so much money/resources at your disposal. When you purchase items you don't need especially exorbitant items you take away resources from the products/services you actually need to purchase (rent, food, transportation). What is the point in buying Jordans or an expensive dress if you have no money to get to work? Basic economic principle and common sense will tell you don't buy what you cannot afford. Saving is an essential part of money management also because this will be the money you use in case of a "rainy day" (believe me a rainy day will come and your savings will show how financially prepared you are.) Most economists agree that if you don't save when you are young chances are you won't save in the future regardless of your increase/ decrease in income. Saving also help making major purchases easier because instead of taking a loan or using a credit card you can use saved money to aid that purchase. Spending and saving are habits. Both can be good or bad spending on your level of financial responsibility and common sense …………..
Now with that said just let that sink in

Just so everyone knows CREDIT CARDS ARE NOT YOUR MONEY. You're spending financial institution money and I always recommend that if you have to use a credit card, do so wisely. Always try to make the full payment and never the minimum. If you pay only the minimum amount due on the bill the total develops interest (that's how companies make money off people). Buy things that you need and more importantly can afford, that way you can pay back easily. Make sure you already have the money put aside for the payment. Too many people over spend and then end up in debt and do utter despicable acts after such as take out credit cards in their children's name(what 5 year old has bad credit?). Also something I feel strongly about never purchase anything expensive with your credit for anyone. It doesn't matter how cool or related you are with and individual, don't play with your financial future. In the event they decide they won't pay you back you're stuck with the bill and you risk damage to your credit (don't put your credit rating in someone else's hand). Women, does it make sense to buy a 400 dollar dress that you only going to wear once and you risk your credit rating because you could not pay it back? Men, does it make sense to buy all the flashy things to get women's attention and the debt collectors ruining your credit? Being responsible with a credit card is a blessing. I'll leave you with this saying "A wiseman will leave his children a will, A spendthrift will leave his children a bill" ……….. Now with that said just let that sink in

Focus you attention on a rather unique but common issue (I'm not sure if that is an oxymoron by the way) …Excuses. There are 3 phrases I have constantly had extinguish out of my vocabulary … I can't, I'm not good enough and I have an excuse. Everyone has an excuse, but the people who are destined for greatness have desires and not only embrace opportunity, but seek to create it. Benjamin Franklin was quoted once saying "He that is good for making excuses is seldom good for anything else." I have these 2 friends I will not name but every time I have an event they always show up regardless of time, date, weather condition and I appreciate that. On one of their birthdays I was supposed to go to their birthday party but I was really tired from work and too tired to drive and I thought maybe I should stay home. However I decided not to make an excuse and not to disappoint the people who support me in my endeavors. Excuses are always easy to make. I know we all may have extraordinary situations and emergencies and that is understandable but a lot of time excuses become the fabric of our nature. Broken promises, guarantees that were supposed to be good has gold, no shows etc… are all backed up by an excuse. Today I want to encourage everyone to start embracing opportunities, start honoring your word/promises/guarantees and avoid using excuses as the easy way out … give you self a chance to embrace opportunity and play a part in not disappointing yourself or someone you respect..............Now with that said just let that sink in

I seek to encourage you to make time for positivity. Never say you don't have time to engage in activities that will benefit you. You can always make time. If the president of the United States of America can make time then you can do also. I will explain how. Let me use myself as an example... I am an avid sports video game fan and I like to relax and spend time playing video games however, I realized the time I spent play video games I could actually spend that time positively enhancing myself e.g. reading positive books, going to the gym, writing my daily affirmations, listening to motivational speeches etc... I know these are central to obtain my goals/dream of being a positive/motivational speaker. Every opportunity you have to make progress, you should take advantage of undoubtedly. The bodybuilder doesn't get huge muscles by only going to the gym when he feels like it... he invest his free time in the gym and in himself. We can always make time. Invest time in positive activities and you will enhance yourself. Today I desire to stimulate your mind to grasp the concept of positive living in your recreation activities. Whatever you invest you free time in can be the x-factor in your progress in life. The greatest investment you can make is in yourself.............. Now with that said just let that sink in

Let's talk about having big dreams. Firstly, let me tell you when you have big dreams people will tell you that you are crazy. Some will even try to discourage you. My humble advice is to not let them get to you. Don't be surprised when people don't go along with your dreams and find all kind of reasons to show you how it will not work. Many of today's inventions and ideas all started by individuals with great dreams …E.g. Facebook, the telephone, the automobile, locomotives, airplanes, the internet… etc. Your dreams should always be big. Always aspire to make the impossible possible. Visualize the end result in your mind and keep up with your daily motivation working towards it. When you have big dreams/goals/aspirations you are saying to yourself "I can and I will". Thomas Edison one of the greatest inventors when he was asked by a reporter about his unsuccessful attempts at many inventions quipped up this response "I haven't failed. I just found 10000 ways that won't work." You to have what I call "continuous optimism." That term simply suggests that regardless of what setbacks you have your desire for success must be undeterred. I personally try to use anything and look for a positive in going after my dreams. I believe fairy tales can even be a source of inspiration in accomplishing big dreams because they show us the unbeatable dragons can be conquered. Today I want to leave you with this quote I wrote a while ago "Believe in yourself and in your dreams because they are the brainchild of your imagination and represent the conceptualization of your thinking" … now with that said just let that sink in.

In today's world a lot of people are blaming the younger generation for society's problems. This couldn't be further from the truth. A lot of issues today started with the older generation and I make no beans about it, also I will seek no armistice- agreement to retract to that statement. Let me give some examples. A father gives his 15 year old son his first taste of alcohol and after a while he starts to equate alcohol with manhood. So drinking is something that men do (at least this is what he has been taught) possibly starting him down the road of being an alcoholic. A video store owner whose business has become a teenage boy's hangout has a "backroom video section" where teens can purchase sexual explicit material, sowing the seeds of a possible sexual deviance/perversion. Politicians argue, lie and steal in full view of the public eyes and young people see this, realize and throw their morals/honesty/integrity out the window because of the "perceived way of the world" is to be selfish and dishonest. Fathers abandon their children because of a disagreement with their kids' mother thus leading to a household without a father figure and a proper example for his sons of how to be a man, eventually adopting an idea of a man propagated by the media and peer pressure. The end result is we produce young people without character, discipline, integrity and a generation which shun and belittles those who have morally sound fundamentals. I want everyone reading this to look at the example they are setting for the young people. Remember they are only doing what they were taught to do and what they were exposed to. Teach them the right type of propaganda such as: love, respect, humility, integrity, honesty, dedication and the list goes on. If you don't, then you have no right to criticize the youths because the finger (hopefully not a gun) is pointing at you ……now with that said just let that sink in

I will like to share a simple story which happened in early 2014. Because of my torrid work schedule I usually don't get time to go to the laundry as I would like so I started dropping off my laundry to a certain Laundromat (I won't call the name). At first the people working there were friendly and everything was cool. One day I picked up my clothing and to my horror and surprise a lot of my clothes had bleach spots on them. So I immediately went to the Laundromat and explained to the lady, before my clothes were brought here they never had any bleach spots on them (ever). The lady watched me in my face and started lying saying it wasn't their fault. On top of lying she insisted maybe I have bleach in my house and it got on the clothing. The funny thing is that I am allergic to bleach so all my life I have never been around it (not even the smell I can take). I promptly told her this and her face was shell-shocked. Even though I caught her in a lie I was still willing to work out some sort of compensation with her but she kept on lying. I stopped going to that place and found a new Laundromat which treats me much better, knows me by name, drying is free and is very personalized with service. My point being, honesty is the always the best policy. If that lady at the other Laundromat had been honest I might have still been a customer there. Her lying cost her my business and there is no telling how many other people she may have lied to and lost customers. Lying always never works out and it is not a trait to develop with consistency. No one is perfect but especially in a business sense I quote WWE Superstar Triple H "it is not what's best for business" ……..now with that said just let that sink in

A Simple scenario: One morning I decided to the take the highway on my daily commute, while driving, there was a huge pothole in the road, unfortunately for me I didn't see it because a huge trailer was directly in front of me so I had the most uncomfortable dip into a pothole I have ever experienced. The wheel swerved a little and then came back on course and I continued along my merry way to my destination. After checking the vehicle and reading the manual what I didn't know is that the vehicle is designed to combat situations like that. The people who manufactured the vehicle give it a "bounce-back" ability (the suspension coils). Today regardless of what potholes are placed in your life don't allow them to stop your progress. You too have that "bounce-back" mentality installed within you. All you have to do is realize it. God gave you the ability to overcome all situations and setbacks whether they are emotional/ social/spiritual/mental/ physical etc….. Too many of us encounter scenarios and we just stop trying. I would know because I was one of those people. Hard situations/tests help develop character to aid you in the long run to overcome the gauntlet of life pitfalls. I want to encourage all of you to not allow any situation overcome your will. You have what it takes to be successful and achieve what your heart desires. If that pothole didn't stop my vehicle this morning then your situation cannot stop you. My SUV was built by men. You were built, designed and constructed by the greatest manufacturer of them all, God almighty…………now with that said just let that sink in

Let me tell you about my doctor. A very humble person and she is one of the friendliest people I have met. Something which she does every year is that when it is anyone in my family's birthday she always sends a birthday card. What I didn't know is that she sends it out to all her patients, which is her way of showing appreciation to her customers (and also it is a very unique gesture and good for business). I appreciate the fact that she go above and beyond just to show appreciation. Regardless of who you are and what you do it is always a good to receive and show appreciation. When one is appreciated it uplifts their spirits and motivates them. Everyone is encouraged by the fact that someone recognized their existence has special. I once read of a study that 3 billion people on the earth will go to bed hungry for food but more than 4 billion (more than half the planet's population) will go to bed longing for some sincere appreciation. Whether it is at home, school, work, church, community organizations everyone should show appreciation to each other. The Perpetual Calendar of Inspiration (inspired by Vera Nazarian), states "Love is made up of three unconditional properties in equal measure Acceptance, Understanding, Appreciation..." In essence when you appreciate people you are expressing love ....now with that said just let that sink in

I want to teach a different type of martial arts skill. It is called mental self-defense. It can work on you and it can work on others. Let me give you an example. When I was in my teenage years I played a lot of football (soccer) and in one game I was playing the striker position. I had an opportunity to pass the ball to another player but instead I decided to shoot the ball towards goal. It was a bad decision as the ball sailed over the crossbar and we ended up tying the game. The next day a group of older guys all started heckling and using vile words telling me how useless I was and that I should stick to books. I responded by saying "yes I may have made a bad play but at least I tried what did you do?" I even reminded them that while I was playing they were just spectators and I even borrowed a line from WWE hall of Famer The Rock and told them "It doesn't matter what they think" especially seeing that they weren't my teammates. I even later recorded a song about the incident called "Criticize." My point being, I defended my mind and my thought processes from the negative attacks by responding with positive counter-attack. While they tried to show up my failures I showed up my ability to focus on the positive in the situation. In today's world negativity is the order of the day but the good thing is that you don't have to subscribe to it. Practice your mental self-defense techniques and become the Bruce Lee of fighting against negative words, thoughts and expressions gestured towards you…. now with that said just let that sink in

Let's talk about having the right type of people in your life. If you have someone in your life that supports your dreams, encourages you at every opportunity and they invest time and resources into you being a success, hold on to them. If they constantly give you positive criticism, that person is an individual who truly deserves a special place in your life. These type of people are rare and literally worth their weight in gold. These precious people you have in your life are the human forms of gems, diamonds and pearls because they help you to realize your value and potential. In a world of too many wolves in sheep's clothing it is nice to know when you have someone who is unconditionally in your corner it is a blessing. I once told someone before in general terms of speaking the only two characters that will love and defend you unconditionally is your mother and your dog.....if you find someone else that does that, consider it a privilege and honor to have such a person in your life and don't be afraid to express appreciation to them for being such a person....now with that said just let that sink in

I was watching a national geographic wild special and I saw something interesting that I figured we can learn from. A group of meerkats(a member of the moogoose family) was walking cross the kalahari desert in Botswana and out of nowhere a lion –the king of the beast came across their path. One would think that a lion should make short work of a group of meerkats but think again. The meerkats sensing the danger banded-tightly together to repel the lion and not one of them was harmed. The mightiest of beast was forced to abandon his supper plans for them. Point being there is strength not just in numbers but also in unity. The lion was stronger and would outweigh them combined but unity is what kept them alive. When we unite we can accomplish more than we would individually and goals become easier. The dream becomes a reality. Teamwork and unity helped that clan of meerkats to live another day imagine what it can do for us as humans...... now with that said just let that sink in

Let me help you understand why thinking negative is bad for you. Let's use an example from the animal kingdom. Termites are extremely small creatures but they have a taste for wood. Termites can multiply quickly and soon they can destroy any surface that is made of wood. In the same way negative thoughts can multiply and destroy an individual's self esteem. The dollar value of the termites' devastation can run into millions unless treated. Similarly, if negative thoughts remain with an individual the damage can affect them in ways which can be disastrous (physically/emotional/spiritually)... Today I encourage you not to let any negative thoughts harbor itself in your mind, regardless of how small it is.... Reject the negative thoughts and start embracing the positive ideas...there hasn't been any negative ideas which have gotten anyone further in life....now with that said just let that sink in

Let me show you something: In today's world all that is depicted throughout various forms of mass media are lies, deceit, unnecessary drama, chaos, fighting and backstabbing (check the popular TV shows/movies) just to name a few. Whether we want to admit or not, the media affects our minds subconsciously. A precise but unfortunate reflection of society. Our minds are being flooded with such and people unfortunately want to act out what they see. I advise you to guard your mind on what you spend your time viewing. The effects can be permanent …..Now with that said just let that sink in

Let's look at this from a logical and mathematical standpoint. If you are in a situation which you are unhappy about but you refuse to come out of the situation how do you expect things to change? Mathematics teaches us unless we change the variables of an equation the answer will always be the same. 2+2=4 everyday of the week. The only time that changes, is when a variable is removed, added or the sign changes. If you are unhappy with your life I suggest that you look at your life's equation and make necessary change/s so that the result will be different……………..…. now with that said just let that sink in

I am writing this to let you know that regardless of what anyone tells you that you are awesome. You are special. Almighty God took time out to create and design you in his image. You are the highest form of life. When God made you he put something special in you. The bible says that "we are wonderfully and fairly made" and that we were "created in his image and likeness". You heard that! You were designed on his blueprint. The human mind and body are wonders. Go to the mirror, look at yourself and see the uniqueness God has given you. ....now with that said just let that sink in

Before we attempt to fix or correct others mistakes we should learn to correct our own flaws. Furthermore we should learn to accept criticism especially if it is positive. A lot of times we want to talk but seldom listen and do retrospectives. If you are in the process of becoming a better person your will accept, respect and be amicable to positive criticism. God gave you one mouth but two ears: a subtle divine sign that you listen twice as much as you speak. You already know what you are doing right, now it's time you know what you're doing wrong and what can be improved. The people I value most are those who are not afraid to tell me what I am doing wrong and how I can improve. Once you begin to accept and love constructive criticism you are on the road to becoming a better individual ....now with that said just let that sink in

The beaver is quite a remarkable animal in terms of an engineering standpoint. It is one of the few animals which have the ability to affect its environment and change nature's landscape literally. It can turn small streams and tributaries into massive ponds creating a stable home for not only itself but also other animals by simply constructing a dam. It is not influenced by its environment but rather it is an innovator in altering the environment. Today I want to encourage you to create the right environment for yourself. Your environment does not shape you but rather you have the tools necessary just like the beaver to alter your environment. Make a change in your life for the better and stop living in the status quo reflection of your environment. Whether it means reading books, changing your friends, putting in extra on work etc... Do what you must to take the lead in changing your life's landscape. Take a hint from the beaver and be an innovator and affect change.............now with that said just let that sink in

One of the most important characteristics we can develop as human beings is patience. Believe you me that was something I had to learn... Patience is a quality that can and should be worked on....a personal example is that some time ago I was having car trouble so I went to the mechanic at 9am... apparently the problem with my vehicle required at least 5 hours work. And it actually took longer than that time. I didn't have breakfast and I was frustrated with the timeframe. However, I took that time to occupy my mind with re-affirming positive thoughts and before I knew it the work was completed and I was satisfied. Years ago I would have gotten angry, yelled or complained. Acting that way doesn't make any process go any faster, so why do it? Today I charge you if you are impatient like I used to be, when placed in a situation which requires patience try to plan for it: carry a book or two for reading, games on your cell phone (walk with your charger) etc… being proactive can play a part in helping you develop this skill……now with that said just let that sink in

Too many people in the world today are seeking instant gratification. The problem with this is that almost nothing in life is worth instant gratification. It is not the natural order of things. E.g. when a baby is born it does not have the ability to walk immediately. ..First he learns to rollover, and then he might learn to sit up, then crawl, then stand up, then walk with assistance and finally walk unassisted. Here you see a clear process of steps and learning taking place. With instant gratification the proper procedures are not followed and rush decisions result in some of the following outcomes…unwanted pregnancy, jail/prison time, mismanagement of money etc. The point is, if you try to skip the necessary steps you would not learn the lessons required to help you grow. The idea of steps and processes take place in all facets of life. When you try to skip them you are only putting yourself at a disadvantage the outcomes can be permanent …now with that said just let that sink in

Question. How would you in your right mind lock yourself in a room with the following: venomous snakes, Alligators, poisonous spiders, and grizzly bears? If the answer is no, then why so? Because they are all very dangerous and will most definitely cause harm /serious injury. It would completely make sense to avoid them. The same way you should avoid toxic people. These people have nothing to offer you and will only aid you to dismember your goals and aspirations. Too many times people associate with individuals/cliques that they know are not good for them. If you have a friend that steals it won't be long before they try to convince you to steal. If you spend time with the wrong people you will become like them. They seek to influence you in things that you know you have no business doing. Whether it is using drugs, stealing, fighting, disrespecting women, drinking or thinking negatively, they will impact you. Today I want to encourage you to avoid those people like you would a grizzly bear. Toxic people can and will infiltrate your mind if you continue to associate with them. It is just a matter of time ....now

I want to write about counting your blessings. One time my father told me of a story about a guy who was on his last... (He had no desire to live due to his life being so messed up). He was going to eat his last banana and then kill himself. After eating the banana he threw away the banana peel. Suddenly, out of nowhere a homeless person dove and caught the banana peel in mid air and started to eat it. The guy seeing this realized that his life could be much worst and subsided his planned suicide ....Moral of the story is, no matter how bad it is with you there is always someone wishing that they had what you have. Stop complaining and be grateful and appreciate the things you have…………….now with that said just let that sink in.

I want to just encourage anyone going through tough times. It is not over until you overcome it. Tough times help to make us stronger. Please don't give up. You are not a quitter. When I was going through the rough and tough times in my life I was reminded of this saying "Smooth seas never made a skilled sailor". The tough times will only help to strengthen you. Keep your head up and continue fighting the good fight. You are bigger than the situation. Here are 4 Keys to help you overcome the circumstances: Continuous Optimism, Long term vision, Hard-work and Faith/Prayer. Usually all these elements are combined in any over comer's arsenal. You have already won…..This too shall pass…….. …remember that ………now with that said just let that sink in.

A have a quick question for you. If you where to drive your car and you got a flat tire would you leave the car there at the side of the road and get out and go back to the where you came from? NO! You might get out and change the tire yourself, call a tow truck, call a friend for help or do something to fix the car so you can keep on moving to get to your destination. So why do so many people in pursuit of their dreams/goals pull over turn around and forgo their cause? Don't let minor setbacks dissuade you from continuing to make progress. When trying to accomplish anything you will encounter setbacks. That is a part of the process. No single invention/ idea was successful on a first attempt. Once you find a solution, you can get moving and continue making progress. I plead with you today; don't abandon your dreams just because of a setback. Keep moving forward………..now with that said just let that sink in.

I want to encourage you to keep your faith in going after your dream. There is a popular biblical scripture which says "Faith is the substance of things hoped for, the evidence not seen". So true. When you believe in something you can envision it without a physical replication present. Why is that? Because you have already seen it with you heart, mind and soul. Every inventor who developed a product saw it before it was manifested in a tangible form. Every accomplishment starts off with the belief that it can be done. When you have nothing and you believe anything is possible your faith is manifested. Go forward with your faith believe that once you continue putting the time /work /effort that your dreams can become a reality………..now with that said just let that sink in.

Here is my remedy for dealing with the hater. Now it can be a tricky task but I believe if executed properly and you follow my instructions you will master it. Step 1: Ignore, Step 2: Repeat Step 3: Repeat steps 1 & 2…………now with that said just let that sink in.

Here is a synopsis… Let's say you had a world class, million dollar race horse …The kind to win the Kentucky derby or the Belmont stakes would you keep him up all night, feed him beer and pizza, stop him from racing or teach that horse to smoke ? Of course you wouldn't because that horse is valuable. So why then would you treat you body in such a way. You are more precious than that horse but yet Too many of us treat our possessions better than we would treat our own selves. You won't allow someone to smoke or drink in your car but a lot of people out there are smoking and drinking themselves to death. People would spend thousands of dollars on the up keep or a car but won't spend 20 dollars on healthy food or a gym membership. Today I want to encourage everyone reading this to start taking better care of your bodies. Make better dietary choices. A positive mind combined with a healthy diet is a great scenario to have. God gave you this body and it is your responsibility to maintain it …..Now with that said just let that sink in.

Drinking is not necessary for you to have a good time. Question what is so good about drinking to the point of getting incoherent and hung-over? Some people make the argument that alcohol helps to take the edge off. Non-sense. It simply gets you intoxicated so that you think the edge is off. If alcohol is so good then why do the doctors discourage pregnant women from drinking or why don't we have alcohol in baby formulas or why does the government spend millions of dollars in campaigns saying don't drink and drive. There is absolute correlation between fun and alcohol however there is a link between alcohol and illness/death. Sorry to burst you bubble …actually I'm not sorry... Proverbs 20 verse 1 states "Wine is a mocker, strong drink is raging and whosoever is deceived thereby is not wise"……… now with that said just let that sink in.

Let me say this… it is better to move on with your life than seek closure. Sometimes you have to leave things and just get up and go on. Too many of us are stuck on the how's and why's of circumstances for things that happened 5, 10 and even 20 years ago. Some people will never give you closure. So what if you didn't get a reason why, that apology or that last conversation? A lot of times that closure is not worth it. Learn to move on with your life. The past has already happened. Focus on your future and work to make it better. Be positive and keep on looking forward and up...............now with that said just let that sink in

Just an encouragement to everyone to be kind to everyone you meet. Many people out there are fighting battles that we have no idea about. You can be the person to help that individual recover. Your kindness is never wasted. Be kind, courteous and humble. Attributes we should all aspire to have………now with that said just let that sink in

If you had a rough time last week, I just want to push you mind to focus on the upcoming week. Forget the rough week and concentrate on future. Always keep that futuristic mindset. This will help you to move on and seek to make the most of the time you have…..now with that said just let that sink in

Never let anyone make you believe that you are too young or too old to do anything. Age has never been a factor in establishing, pursuing or accomplishing goals. Too many people are allowing themselves to get put down because of age. Regardless of your age do not be deterred in pursing goals. It doesn't matter what anyone tells you, keep on working and believing in yourself. You are never too young or too old to start. Age is a deterrent to them, not to you. Today you are as good as any to start working on your dreams…… now with that said just let that sink in

Just in case your life is not going the way you planned I got news for you. It can be turned around. Very few situations in life are unchangeable or hopeless. Double and triple your work rate in order to achieve your goals and to put yourself back on the path you want to be. Realize where you are in life is the first step in pursuing your goals. You are able to take stock and begin the process of progress. Whatever it is you want to accomplish set short term goals to attain in pursuit of your long term goals. When you have long term goals short range frustration won't hamper you. Your scenario or situation can be turned around if you would just give full effort and commitment to the cause.............now with that said just let that sink

The Wild dog packs in Africa are some of the most effective hunters in the world. They lack the size and strength of the lion, the power of a hyena, and guile of a leopard and the speed of a cheetah. However, what they do have is the numbers game and endurance on their side. While all the major predators on the continent are bigger than them, they don't look at that but rather stick to their strengths and are quite successful. My point here is stop looking at the qualities of others and start looking at your strengths and work on using them to your advantage. When you learn to develop the skills and resources you have, you will be able to even the playing field in pursuit of whatever your goals are. Start embracing your gifts............. now with that said just let that sink in

The crocodile is one of the most ruthless predators in the animal kingdom. It is also one of the most successful predators and it is known for its patience. It has been known to sometimes observe its prey for between 6 hours to several days before attempting to make the kill. It is the ultimate opportunist in the animal kingdom. What can we learn from this animal? First, we need to learn to develop patience as a character trait, secondly we also need to be ruthless in pursuing our goals, and thirdly we need to take opportunities as they are presented to us. The crocodile is successful because it combines all three of these to its advantage. Today I encourage everyone to follow the croc's example and work on developing and embedding these character traits…now with that said just let that sink in

Regardless of how many "no's" you get in life, don't let that deter you. There is a "yes" somewhere out there in your future. Too many times we let the "no's" make us pack up and go home. Research indicates that the average American male by age 18 would have been told "no" 148000 times. However, I'm a believer in continuous optimism and the possibility of a "yes" in the future. Rejections, denials and rebuffs happen to everyone but you continue working diligently at whatever you are doing and eventually the yes's will become more abundant and frequent…….now with that said just let that sink in

Bad company breeds bad habits, bad habits breed bad character; the same way good company breeds good habits, good habits breed good character. Be mindful of those who you surround yourself with. Watch the dialogue/ conversations, interactions, situations and attitudes of the people you associate with. Whether you like it or not they are a reflection of your intentions. Be careful and be aware………now with that said just let that sink in

Grenada is a small island roughly twice the size of Washington D.C in the southern Caribbean with a population of about 110,000. I have had the pleasure of visiting the island several times and it is a true gem in its own right. The main crop on the island is nutmeg. Grenada is the world 2nd largest producer (25%) of nutmeg behind Indonesia (70%) which has a population that is 2,294 times bigger than them. However, Grenada does not look at its size as limitation or try to compete with Indonesia, rather the nation focuses on developing what it has to maximize output and be a world leader in that particular field. Today, I want to encourage you to focus on doing the best you can with the abilities that you have. Size does not matter but maximizing your potential is what counts......With that said just let that sink in

Let me simply say that we are nothing without God. Riches and accomplishments are nice but at the end of the day it comes down to God's Blessings. There are so many things we are unaware of that God has provided for us and kept us from (both seen and unseen). Acknowledgement of his grace and presence is a key factor in our daily blessings. Keep your soul connected to God and your life will be enhanced. It is nice to appreciate the created but even greater to acknowledge the creator............With that said just let that sink in

I will reveal something to you. The real reason for murder is a lack of respect for God. If you respect the creator you will not seek to kill his creations. You would not seek to engage in malicious activities which can cause death or harm to people if only the respect factor was there for the Almighty. What God made, man has no right to destroy……….. With that said just let that sink in

I was reading an article about the World Fastest man, Usain Bolt and it really captivated my interest. According the website britannica.com from an engineering standpoint, he should not be the fastest man in the world. His body type and long limbs are more suitable for long distance running rather than a short sprinter. His height of 6'5 and size should slow him down as longer limbs are supposed to slow a person down during a race. Try telling that to him. Yet, in spite of this, he continues to break world records at an outstanding rate. Today I want you to forget what the scientists and experts are saying. Forget the critics. Ignore the naysayers. Remember all a critic does is criticize. You go out there, focus on your goals and make it happen……………….. Now with that said just let that sink in

I just want to inform you of a mistake a lot of us make in our lives and I too have made it in the past. Stop evaluating your future based on your current scenario. While the future can be impacted by the present, you have the power to alter your life's course. Too many people hold back on ideas, dreams, aspiration and goals because currently they don't see a way for it to get done. What you can do is assess your current situation and start taking stock on how to make progress so that you can achieve the future you desire. Use your present to invest in your future. Set goals and objectives and start working on them diligently. Every successful person in every area of life has had that in common.............now with that said just let that sink in

Oil companies when they are searching for oil know that it is not a guarantee that every well they drill will be successful. On average 7 out of 8 holes are "dry wells". So why would they (Geologist) keep encouraging drilling if they only had a 1/8 chance of being successful? Here's why, because they believe and know that when they do find oil that it would be worth it regardless of how many unsuccessful dry wells they drilled. Today, regardless of how many attempts you have made, I want to let you know not to give up. You may have to attempt 100 times or you may have to attempt 1000 times but you should continue to believe that whatever you do will be worth it at the end. When you are successful and you accomplish your goals /desired result, you will experience one of the most elated feelings of happiness ever and you have the satisfaction of knowing you didn't give up....now with that said just let that sink in

Whenever it is lunch time I notice a lot of delivery guys coming in to the office bringing meals for people. I decided that I don't want to get my mind into the habit of people bringing stuff for me ... the habit of convenience. Lunchtime I get up and go out the building and get myself some lunch regardless of rain/snow/heat or cold. I wanted to develop within myself a small habit of getting and doing things for myself. If I could do it for smaller things and master it then I would be able to apply it in other areas of my life. Point here, get into the habit of getting up and doing simple things that you can do for yourself and stop residing in comfort zone, waiting on things to be brought or handed to you. Get up and Go.........now with that said just let that sink in

Tim Duncan is one of the most fundamentally sound basketball players the NBA has ever had. He does the basic things and excels at them. He has literally made a career and carved out a nice living for himself by repetition and execution of fundamental skills. When most players fade as they get older he has gotten more efficient. However, if he went for flash before learning the fundamentals, chances are he would not be as successful as he is. Regardless of what you want to do in this life, whether it is to be a profession athlete, lawyer, doctor, and Disc jockey you have to learn the fundamentals in order to be successful. Learn the lessons that need to be learnt so that you can give yourself a better chance of success. Zig Ziglar said "There is no elevator to success. You are going to have to take the stairs" ....now with that said just let that sink in

God has given everyone talent regardless of who you are. It is up to you to find your talent and develop it. Too many of us are not making use of our abilities and talents. God gave you such gifts so that you can use them. There are so many people hiding their talents for whatever reason (Fear, critics, low self esteem)....Use your talent to change the world and embrace the abilities granted to you by God almighty. Don't deny the world of your greatness...One day he will ask you what have you done with the gifts/talents you were given....my friends you will have to give account...now with that said just let that sink in

Reading is fundamental to everyone. If you are going to be successful in any career field you are going to have to read a lot. Reading outside of academic material helps to give you mind the extra knowledge and insight and you can in turn use that to your advantage to help you make advancements in your particular career. Research shows the average person only reads about one book a year. However, if you commit to reading 20 pages a day, you would have read 12, 200page books a year. That is a lot of insight. Reading is one of the greatest investments you can make in yourself. Consume good reading material for your mind…………..now with that said just let that sink in

Your mind is like a broadcasting device and you generally have two stations. Station N and Station P. Station N (Negative) only shows all your failures, reasons why you can't, tragedies, mistakes and pretty much broadcasts all the negative occurrences and experiences that have taken place in your life. Meanwhile Station P (Positive) focuses on opportunities and potential, strengths, personal victories, public success and small but significant blessings that you have received. Today, I want to encourage you to focus on station P because that is the one which will help you see you're worth and realize your true potential. Boot station N off the air reject its broadcast license …………. now with that said just let that sink in

I want to reflect on the biblical story of Joseph. A victim of jealous brothers, he was sold in slavery, ended up in jail, served in the kings court, wrongful accused of attempted rape went back to jail again, rose through the ranks to be the equivalent of a modern Prime Minister in Egypt and when he had the power to punish his brothers for their ill-will towards him, he ended up being the one to ensure their survival in the time of famine. So many lessons can be learned here but I will only focus on one today. Sometimes God puts us in the most uncomfortable situations only to exalt us to a position of power. Your attitude to recognize and trust in God is critical especially when you are at the bottom. God did not forsake Joseph and he will not forsake you. Exercise your faith with continuous optimism and God will indeed hear you and come to your aide. When you get to that position don't forget where God took you from ....With that said just let that sink in

While in the pursuit of something positive you have someone that is trying to persuade you that your positive is a negative avoid that person. Examples are" why you looking for a better job and you have a good one"/" why you always reading or studying so much...you're not Einstein you know"/ "Stop working so hard". People that echo those kinds of sentiments are not conducive to your cause. They are actually trying dumb you down and hold you to their standards. It is better you lose that person than you lose your ambition. I always encourage everyone to follow their hearts desire no matter of weird, unrealistic or whacky it sounds because you will someday have an impact and change the world. Never let anyone attempt to turn your positive desire into a negative reality. ....now with that said just let that sink in

I wish to engage your attention on thinking ahead. A lot of people are deceived into living for the here and now. While I do believe in maximizing one's joyful experiences we must not forgo our future for our present. We need to develop a vision to make the transition towards our future seamless and not regrettable. Start putting things in place so that you can have a base on which to develop your future. Invest in activities such as saving money, education/academic advancement, spiritual/emotional development...etc. the resources you invest in will help shape your future............. now with that said just let that sink in

Squirrel is an animal with the right type of attitude. During the fall months they start storing food recognizing that the winter is coming and food will become less abundant. One of the worst things for a squirrel is to be caught in the middle of winter without any food. The squirrel has the instinct and acumen for survival and will not put its existence in jeopardy. Similarly, the same way we should plan for the rough times in our future by doing the necessary things... Proverbs 20.v4 says "The sluggard will not plow by reason of the cold; therefore shall he beg in harvest and have nothing." Try to lay a foundation in the harvest time of your life so that you will not be caught out in the cold ....now with that said just let that sink in

Dear young people, my advice to you is to stop trying to impress and fit in with friends you know are engaging in wrong and illegal activities. Some of these activities may include but are not limited to fighting/bullying, sexually intimidation / assault, drinking, drug use/drug dealing, violent behavior, skipping school, stealing/ robbery, illegal gambling, etc...usually people who participate in these activities counter the following outcomes. Jail time(incarceration), hospitalization, dismemberment or disability and last but not last an earlier than expected arrival to the cemetery...Take some time and think about it ....now with that said just let that sink in

It is important to keep your morals. Let me give a simple story. Sometime ago I met up with my parents to go grocery shopping. When we got back to my place we realized that we had a desirable item that we had not purchased. It didn't take much thought to decide to take it back. I returned to the store with the item and the workers in the supermarket were surprised I did that. Point being, my moral code is not to take things that I didn't buy or to be dishonest. Even though they made the mistake, I was not going to compromise my morals. Never let opportunity determine your morals....now with that said just let that sink in

One Saturday I was going for a jog/run and I saw this elderly disabled man and his sister having car trouble, I cut my run short and proceeded to give the car a push and it was a long push. After pushing the vehicle a far distance they were so grateful and right in the middle of the street the lady start pronouncing a blessing on me. They believed that I helped them but in all honesty it was them who helped me. I got an intense workout by pushing the vehicle and a nice rush of adrenaline, I got the satisfaction of helping someone in a grave situation and also I got a blessing. I tell you this, not to make myself sound good but to emphasize that if you genuinely help people in their time of need you will get a blessing in return..........now with that said just let that sink in

I wish to focus your attention on establishing and making priorities. "Put first things first". When you are attempting anything you need to understand the order of importance. Get the things done which take precedence then you can focus on the periphery things. Just like Abraham Maslow's "hierarchy of needs" you have the basics which must be satisfied and if those needs are not met it will throw everything else out of order. Too many of us confuse wants and desires for priorities. Get into the habit of setting and more importantly knowing what your priorities are. Misguided priorities are like an assassin's bullet because they will be a dream killer and hamper progress. Therefore, get yourself in order, stay focused and ensure that you are doing "first things first" .... now with that said just let that sink in

I seek to inform you on the two types of thinkers in this world. Complaint based and Solution based. People who have the complaint based thinking normally just identify problems, are generally in unhappy moods, never get anything accomplished and of course complain their way through life's various scenarios. On the other hand, the

Solution Based thinker identifies issues and seeks out ways in which to solve the issues, stop issues from occurring again and is always seeking out ways to develop and improve solutions. They embrace problems as a challenge and in process become innovators in solving them. Today I want to encourage you to avoid being a Complaint based thinker and direct your mind towards a Solution based thought process. All successful people have this character trait ......Now with that said just let that sink in

The Taj Mahal located in Uttar Pradesh, India is one of the most spectacular edifices ever constructed. People come from all over the world to visit this building and it has been a marvel ever since its completion in 1653. However this building and every other man-made structure all started off the same way. A vision and one brick. Today I encourage everyone to get started on manifesting the vision you have for your life. When you have big dreams in order for them to be realized you need to get started. Procrastination is the enemy of success. Start laying the foundation down by doing the simple things you know are necessary for actualization of your dream. The Taj Mahal was someone's dream and it took 22 years to complete. I recommend you get started on yours..........now with that said just let that sink in.

Have you ever had somebody construct a lie about you and it stuck for a while? I'm sure you have. No matter how hard you try to shake it off people still believe it? I have been down that road before. My simple advice to you is to not allow the venom of that lie to circulate in your system for the rest of your life. While it might hurt, living with anger only intensifies the pain. When it happened to me I took a proactive situation towards it. I decided years after the incident to call up the person, tell them that I forgave them, hung up the phone and moved on with my life. That was my anti-venom right there. Eventually the truth will come out. The Building of lies will someday meet the wrecking ball of truth. Proverbs 19.v9 states "A false witness will not go unpunished, and he who breathes out lies will perish" Don't let that lie demolish the rest of your life...... now with that said just let that sink in

One of the most powerful medicines in the world cannot be bought in local pharmacies and drugstores. I will write you a prescription for it not that I am a doctor but I wholeheartedly believe in it. Your prescription today is for daily doses of laughter. According to several studies those who take that prescription daily have less stress, boost the immune system, relaxed muscles, experience decrease in hypertension and have much better self esteem than the grumpy individual. Laughter causes positive rewards for one's physical and mental health. Some research suggests that laughter reduces cortisol (a chemical linked to stress). In the book of Proverbs 15 v 13 it states "A glad heart makes a cheerful face, but by sorrow of heart the spirit is crushed." Find a website with clean jokes or watch a funny video or sitcom. Please fill this prescription for laughter and doesn't worry about an overdose.....now with that said just let that sink in

I was thinking of the nursery rhyme "The itsy-bitsy spider climbed up the water spout, down came the rain and washed the spider out, out came the sun and dried up all the rain and the itsy-bitsy spider climbed up the spout again." I thought to myself the person whoever made up this is a genius. Why? Because technically every time this is sung we are telling kids defacto that every time they have a stumble in life the idea is to get back up again. We too can apply this to our daily lives. When life's circumstances knock us down we should have motivation just like the itsy-bitsy spider and climb back up life's water spout again. Positivity can come in many sources. Today you were inspired by a nursery rhyme ....now with that said just let that sink in

Sometime ago I was talking to a little boy and I asked him what did he want to be when he grows up and he said he wants to be the first astronaut to go to Saturn. So I asked why Saturn and he said "Because no one has ever done it before." So I responded "when you go to Saturn please bring me back a souvenir" Never discourage anyone who dreams and has goals of the impossible. Only small minds discourage grand ideas. Also never allow anyone to discourage you from your ideas. All the people who have had ideas that were supposedly impossible are the ones who changed the world. The airplane, the telephone, the internet, the space rocket etc. were all impossible ideas which today because of someone's "impossible idea" is a daily reality and very commonplace in our society today. Today I encourage you to encourage someone in their ideas regardless of how distant it may seem. Ridiculous ideas are sometimes the best.....Now with that said just let that sink in

I want to talk to you about idleness. I cannot emphasize how important it is for us to keep away from idle conversations, thoughts, interactions, circumstances and people. Usually nothing good comes when you involve yourself in such negativity. Instead, try being proactive with your thoughts and time, especially in your downtime. Always seek to develop and enhance yourself. Reading, budgeting, exercise, uplifting conversation, seeking opportunities and family time are all constructive uses of free time. The activities you engage in during your leisure time say a lot about you. There is a saying "the devil finds work for idle hands" ... Today has no need for the devil....now with that said just let that sink in

Never think because you are not an expert in giving advice that you can't give it. A lot of times we spend more time playing down the impact of our advice. I always tell people while I am no DR. Phil I will not underestimate the power of my advice. Sometimes all that is required is empathy, sympathy, a listening ear, kind heart and a willingness to understand and not criticize. You have good words and the ability to encourage/motivate someone. I do this every single day. Proverbs 27:17 states "Iron sharpeneth iron; so a man sharpeneth the countenance of his friend." This pretty much means you have the ability to impact others around you. Today you may not be a "Dr Phil" but I encourage you not do underestimate the power of your good words. Sometimes God puts the right words in your spirit to speak to someone and it might just be what they need to hear... now with that said just let that sink in

This is a story which occurred in my past. I was teaching someone to drive and I had been teaching them for a couple of months. They just were not getting it. They almost crashed the car; hit a dog and a tree. I got really frustrated. I yelled at the person then I decided maybe if I changed my approach and my tone of voice I might just get the results and the person might just be more receptive to it. Instead of yelling I started encouraging and motivating the person and lowered my voice to a more amicable tone. Immediately I noticed the individual was more relaxed, had greater control of the car and seemed to embrace my instructions. Pretty much I got the desired result. My point is yelling and screaming at someone will almost never get you the results you're trying to accomplish. This applies for everyone. It is always more appropriate to encourage than intimidate..... Now with that said just let that sink in

Necessity creates opportunity. Many times when the stakes are raised in our lives that is when we use what we have to create what we want. The mistake a lot of us make is that when we hit rock bottom we continue looking down when in reality we should focus on looking up. Every bad situation is an opportunity to rise up and make our own way. I honestly believe that in life there are seldom situations with no hope. Look around and see what can be done and go after it and don't do it half way, but do it with all the dedication and ability that you have. I believe and know you will get out of the abyss which you are stuck in. Overcoming obstacles is the ultimate test of character. With God's help, persistence and commitment, you will overcome. There are millions of rags to riches stories and I always recommend writing your own...now with that said just let that sink in.

We all need to learn when to separate ourselves from people who are not respectful of our existence. Some of us allow continuous disrespect and in doing such we are lowering our own self-esteem. When someone has totally broken down the barriers of respect then it is time to end social relations with that person. A lot of us are hanging on to friendships/relationships that are filled with disregard and insults. It stops today. From this moment forward give yourself the respect you deserve and once you do that anyone who interacts with you will give you that level of respect. Don't reward disrespectful actions with friendship/amicability. Walk away or else the disrespect will be never ending. Love yourself enough not to tolerate disrespect ...now with that said just let that sink in

Would you buy a gun and shoot yourself in the leg? Most likely the answer is no. There is a habit which millions of people engage in that are worse than the scenario mentioned above. Smoking cigarettes is one of the most dangerous habits one can adopt. Scarily enough it's legal. When I talk to most smokers and I ask them why they smoke, the answer is usually as a coping mechanism for stress. The reality is that smoking will in the long run gives more stress. I refer to cigarettes as a "cancer stick" but maybe I should start referring to them as disease sticks. Hypertension, heart problems, lung cancer etc are just a few of the long term health issues that smokers face. Even insurance companies charge higher premiums for smokers as opposed to non-smokers. Today I encourage you do drop this habit or better, never start. Do yourself a favor and take good care of your body. If you wouldn't desecrate your house then you shouldn't do it to you body. .. Now with that said just let that sink in

Every day I have the pleasure and absolute honor to meet regular people and encourage them regardless of their background. They have a multitude of issues but I learned a long time ago you have to see the potential in people. A wise man once said "Treat a man as he is and he will remain as he is but treat a man like he should be and he will become what he should be." Don't see people for their faults. Start seeing and speaking positivity to them. I love rags to riches stories and it would be good knowing I had a part to play in someone's story. How you see, treat and interact with people you think is "beneath" you says a lot more about you than them. So going forward I just want to tell everyone not to judge people based on their past but rather direct them towards a positive future. Don't underestimate the impact of your words. If someone didn't see my potential I would not be able to post this.... now with that said just that sink in

Japan is a nation on a volcanic archipelago located in the Far East Asia and has the world's 10th largest population of 126 million people. However, surprisingly, Japan has absolutely no natural resources of any significance but still they are the world's leader in automobile production and technology. Also they have some of the world biggest oil refineries, steel plants and the 4th largest economy in the world. How is this possible? Back in the late 1960's the government at the time decided that they would set goals to become economic world leaders and they accomplished them by using the one resource they did have. Ingenuity. The Japanese people are some of the most creative in the world and used such to develop their nation and the result is a high standard of living and economic prosperity. Today I encourage you to follow this example, develop and use your creativity/ingenuity to achieve your goals. Don't worry about what you don't have but use your resources/abilities to your advantage. They are more valuable than you think...now with that said just that sink in

Recently, I had one of the most beautiful experiences in my life. I received a phone call from a friend who I have not seen in 15 years. The conversation was filled with delightful memories, love, well wishes, positive reinforcement and of course catching up. Not one single word was uttered about any negative scenarios either one of us are facing. When that conversation was finished the feeling was very euphoric. Ephesians 4:29 states" Let no unwholesome word proceed from your mouth, but only such a word as is good for edification according to the need of the moment, so that it will give grace to those who hear." Have delightful conversations and avoid deceitful dialogue. Too many phone calls are filled with gossip, hate, complaining, back-stabbing and deceit. May your phone conversations be filled with happy words....... now with that said just let that sink in

As a tribute to all the mothers out there I will share one of my childhood experiences. When I was about 8 years old there was an old drunk guy who was giving out money to children. Obviously, it wasn't the right thing to do but my friends and I on the urging of other adults took the paltry amount of $2 from him. When I got home I immediately went to the shop and bought some biscuits and my mother started questioning me about where I got money from. I eventually confessed and she did something that I will never forget. She made me open all the biscuits and throw them away. My mother then explained to me why it was wrong and the various dangers that it could have lead to. Good parenting. The job of a mother is never ending and you have to teach your kids the right qualities from young. Proverbs 22:6 states "Train up a child in the way he should go: and when he is old, he will not depart from it." Respect to all the mothers who take care of their kids not just financially/ physically but also emotionally/morally/ spiritually...now with that said just let that sink in

This mother's day weekend was not as eventful as I had hoped but rather it was regrettable. My family decided to go to a nice upscale restaurant. I had been to the restaurant before and the service is usually exceptional. However, this time it wasn't a pleasurable experience. We were there on time for our reservation and seated quickly however we were there for 90 minutes without service and

I received some of the lamest excuses I have heard from a manager. So after seeing my mother visibly disappointed we just took our food to go. I realized that while this experience was unpleasant I have had much more pleasant experiences there than unpleasant. Yes I will go to that restaurant again. Why? You ask. Too many times in life we focus on the one wrong and ignore all the times those around us got it right. Today I encourage you not to focus on the one error but on your general experience in relating to people. There is no person /organization/business that hasn't dropped the ball before. Try concentrating on character /reputation and not on the mistake….now with that said just let that sink in

Tony Blair Former Prime Minister of the UK once used words to this extent "The British people would laud a great decision, dislike a bad decision but they will have no respect for indecision." Well I agree 100%. Indecision is one of those traits that stop us from committing to a goal and hence halting success. Fear of failure is associated with indecision. I would faster respect someone who tried and failed rather than someone who failed to try. At the end of the day indecision has less reward than mediocrity. Going forward you always analyze your options and commit to whatever it you wish to do. How would you like the following people were indecisive... Your bus driver, Doctor, Pilot, etc...If you would not like it for those persons then you should not like it for you......With that said just let that sink in.

I am going to use my favorite food to bring a point across. Roti (A Trinidadian curried dish of East Indian origin) my absolute favorite food in the entire world. When I start to think about it my mind already visualizes it. It is almost like I can taste, smell, feel and see it before I actually have it on my plate. When I am feeling for it I am ruthless in pursuit of it until I am able to have it in my possession ready to be consumed. Why? Because I have that hunger for it. This is the same ruthlessness and desire you should have when you are pursuing your goals and dreams. You must be able to feel it, envision it and embrace it before you actually have it. Just the very thought of it must get your spirit excited. Don't just set a goal but also develop a hunger for it.........now with that said just let that sink in.

Ray Allen, a 10 time NBA All-star, 2 time NBA champion, the 2001 3-point shootout champion and the NBA's all time leader in 3-pointers made him have had quite a career that most other basketball players would envy. The respect of teammates and opponents alike, he is one of the best. However, what is not commonly known is that he suffers with Obsessive Compulsive disorder (a type of anxiety disorder). However, this has worked to his advantage because one of the side-effects of this a constant need for repetition. It has led to him developing a unique shooting style and one of the quickest releases of any player. He is almost impossible to block when shooting because of this. The lesson here is to not let your so-called disabilities hold you back but rather use them innovatively to create that little extra niche for you to make yourself exceptional… now with that said just let that sink in.

When you are driving a vehicle you most focus on what is in front of you. On occasions you will use your rear-view and side mirrors to check for what's coming up behind you. To make progress in life you have to mostly focus on the goals ahead of you. Only look back to acknowledge mistakes and learn from them. The reason why a lot of people are making no progress in life is because they living in the past and not taking the forward steps towards their future. I encourage everyone to starting looking at life via the windshield and stop wholly focusing on the rearview mirror….. One of my favorite songs from Country and western group Desert Rose Band has the Chorus "one step and two steps backs, nobody gets too far like that". True words ………now with that said just let that sink in.

Let me share something about my daily life with you. In the office where I am, just like any other we have a janitor. Friendly guy and quite a character. I developed a habit where I would take the trash out of the bin and place a new bag so all he has to do is collect it. You might say "that is his job, why are you doing that?" The reason I do it is to remind myself that I am not too big to do a menial task. I am not above anything or anyone. I do this as a self-developmental trait to aid in building my character. Today I ask you to see yourself as a never-ending project and continuously try to develop yourself. Consciously working on yourself is the best project you invest time in. Take pride in this project….now with that said just let that sink in.

During the blizzard of 2015, the parking lot at my work building had a lot of cars which were snowed in. While digging out my car from the snow, I saw a lady there who was struggling to get the snow off her vehicle. So my co-worker and I offered our assistance and eventually we got her car out and pushed it so it can gain traction on the icy road. She came up to us and offered $20. I refused outright and she insisted again but I refused again. My co-worker wasn't so generous and took the money. After she left he asked me why I didn't take it. I told him that I could never charge someone for doing good deed. I considered it an opportunity to help someone. Hebrews 13:16 states "Do not neglect to do good and to share what you have, for such sacrifices are pleasing to God", I guess I am not a very good capitalist, but I will rather be a better human being. Now with that said just let that sink in.

Let say you were a gambling man and you had two dogs. The first dog you fed everyday very healthily and the second dog you barely fed at all, maybe once every 3 days. Put them in a pulling competition against each other which one would you bet on to win? Certainly the dog that is better fed. The same way it is with your mind. Whatever you feed into your mind is what will dominate you. Whether you feed your mind positive or negative the results will be manifested in your life. We all have to be careful of what we allow in our minds. Feed yourself thoughts of positivity, self confidence and inspiration….. now with that said just let that sink in.

A lot of times you hear a lot of speakers talk about the importance of forgiveness. While I do agree it is necessary in the process of emotional healing, nobody addresses those who dished out the hurt. Well today I am targeting my sights on those who committed such an infraction. It seems like they get away Scott-free. Why won't you apologize? Why won't you acknowledge your part in hurting someone? Is your ego too big? Are the words I'm sorry too hard for you to pronounce? You already know what they say about karma. Whether you think you were right in your actions is irrelevant. You hurt someone the least you can do, if you're a decent human being is offer an apology. Life is a circle and what goes around will come around. Anyone who refuses to offer a sincere legitimate apology unfortunately lacks moral fiber…Don't be that person. No one has ever died from an apology…now with that said just let that sink in.

I hear the youth using a term called by the acronym YOLO which means "you only live once". While I have no problem with slangs, just that every time it is used it is followed by some counterproductive and risky behavior. I do believe in maximizing opportunities and making sure the day in itself was well spent why live your life and run the risk of ruining it. Dr John Maxell (professional speaker and pastor) once stated "You can spend your life anyway you want but you can only spend it once." When making choices always think about the road ahead and around the bend. Yes this is your life, but also remember your choices will affect you and maybe others for the rest of your life….now with that said just let that sink in.

Mediocrity is one of the worst human traits we can have. The sad part is that it is so easy to develop but hard to break out of. Staying in the status quo is the normal thing to do. Mediocrity actually doesn't take a lot of effort. Settling, just getting by, not actively trying to make progress are all signs of mediocrity. Well I got news for you. I know you can and will do better. How you may ask? Get out of the habit of settling. Successful people never put themselves in a position to be comfortable. Today the bell of excellence has been rung. Time to get up and put your talents to work. Warriors never go into battle with dull axes and swords, but rather they always keep their weapons battle ready. Same way we should keep ourselves sharp in the battle against mediocrity. It's an easy battle to lose..... Now with that said just let that sink in.

We live in what I consider the entitlement age. Seems like people no longer want to work for anything. Young and old. Rich and poor, it doesn't seem to matter. The prevailing mentality is society seems to be "you owe me this", "I deserve that", "gimmie this" or "I am entitled to this". Whatever happened to working hard for what you want? Teenagers demanding their parents buy them a car when they turn 16 or people demanding that society owes them certain luxuries. It's time we start recognizing we are not owed anything in life. Get the thought in your mind that if you want something that you should go out and work for it. The mindset of entitlement flows downstream to the lake of laziness. Humor writer Mark Twain put it this way The world owes you nothing. It was here first. Mark Twain Rid yourself from this mental plague and seek out innovative ways in which to obtain what you desire..........Now with that said just let that sink in.

Let's look at the Biblical story of Noah and the Ark. God instructed Noah to construct the ark because the sea was going to flood the earth due to man's evil ways. The critics laughed, mocked and scorned Noah especially knowing that it had not rained for many years. After 120 years a flood finally came and the rest is history. There is no such thing as planning too early. Planning is what makes all the difference in your future. It doesn't matter what the critics say about your planning. Formulating a plan for your future is one of the best things anyone can do. I'll leave you with this quote from time management author Alan Lakein "Planning is bringing the future to the present so you can do something about it now"...now with that said just let that sink in.

Here is my recipe for baking cookies. Eggs, water, flour/cookie dough, milk, sugar, chocolate chips, sprinkle and the secret ingredient, cow dung. If I offered you these cookies would you eat them? Of course not. Why because the quality has been compromised. The same way it is with our morals. When you compromise your morals you are changing the very dynamic which is you. You willing be creating yourself as a sub-standard product. Any smart person would not disvalue themselves. Instead I encourage you to build yourself as superior brand. If you wouldn't settle for those cookies mentioned before, you should never entertain any sort of compromise when it comes to your morals.........now with that said just let that sink in.

Steve Fossett is an American millionaire, but he is mostly known as one of the few people to travel around the world via a hot air balloon. In 1997 during his travels, he was denied permission to travel in Libya's airspace but his hot air balloon was headed straight on course for Libya. It was likely they would shoot him out of the sky, in effort to avoid this Fossett came up with a plan. He decided to lower his altitude so that he could catch a wind current to help him avoid a possible fatal outcome. In the end, he mildly touches the nation's southern border avoiding an international incident. Sometimes in life we have to take our heads out of the clouds in order to make progress. Changing our mental altitude will lead us achieving things with a better attitude. Don't feel because you are way up there in terms of status, you are too good to lower your ego to accomplish anything. Steve Fossett learned this and I hope we all will as well…. Now with that said just let that sink in.

I once heard a businessman say, "I have over 20 years experience in doing this, so I don't need to do any research. I am the research". Any business investment with this individual is a bad investment. Why? Because anytime someone is unwilling to change and is a know-it-all, that shows they won't take the time to do want is necessary. They believe they have all the answers. A massive misguided ego. No one has all the answers. 1 Corinthians 3:19 states "For the wisdom of this world is foolishness with God. For it is written, He taketh the wise in their own craftiness." Anyone who thinks too highly of himself to learn something still has a lot more to learn. Smart people learn continuously so that improvements and advancement can be made. Follow the path of continuously learning…..now with that said just let that sink in.

One of the things I love about myself is that I am teetotaler. That's right I don't drink alcohol. I am actually pretty proud of myself. I can walk in social and professional gathering and not even be tempted by the availability of alcohol. I have been to bars before but never even felt the urge to take a sip. Some people often find it strange that I don't take a drink or even suggest that it might loosen me up / take the edge off. Guess what? I am already drunk from positivity, success and self confidence. I don't need any substance to make me feel good. Proverbs 20.1 "Wine is a mocker, strong drink is raging: and whosoever is deceived thereby is not wise." When you rely on substances that is an indication something is missing from your life. Whatever you looking for I guarantee you won't find it there…..now with that said just let that sink in.

One thing that stops me from buying goods in a store is when I see a sign that says" All sales are final, No refunds, only exchange." That to me says the business owner does not have full confidence is his products. It is almost like they are telling you "bad products, your problem not mine," I prefer businesses that will freely refund you if you have a legitimate issue with their product because it portrays to me that they believe in their product and believe in good ethics. Any business which has good ethics will make more money than one which has that no refund /exchange only policy because they will retain more customers...now with that said just let that sink in.

When I go to clean my car I developed a business relationship with the guy who washes the vehicle named OG (I don't know his real name). However one Saturday I requested OG and he was not feeling well and they told me he was resting. I was genuinely concerned about him so I checked up on him. I don't see him as the man who cleans my car but as a human being with feeling/emotions. OG was very pleased; he appreciated my concern about his welfare and insisted on washing the car. Start seeing people as people and not as their occupation....now with that said just let that sink in.

Some people describe themselves as just going with the flow. I never really liked that kind of thinking. Reason being is that it doesn't indicate a clear defined set of goals. It is what I call the "plastic bag in the wind" theory. No clear direction, ambition or focus these people usually just follow trends, accept any outcome and miss out on opportunities. The people that accomplish things in life will tell you that they had a vivid idea of what they wanted to do and actively pursued them. To avoid being a follower of the plastic bag theory get a pen and paper and start writing down your goals and begin working towards it......now with that said just let that sink in.

A real-life example of why to stay away from negative and disrespectful people. I have a friend who always goes around happy-go-lucky. However, he kept having non-essential contact with a negative, disrespectful individual on his job which always ended in a confrontation. I told him on numerous occasions to avoid the individual and stop trying to keep that individual front and center. He explained to me that he can't keep grudges and I told him it was not about grudges but it was about letting go of the negative/disrespectful people in your life. He still insisted on keeping contact with the individual. Less than 2 weeks later, he and that individual had a confrontation that almost became physical and it was in full view of the company's senior director. End result..? They both got fired on the spot. I am of the belief that his constant excuses to associate with negativity cost him a job. I encourage you to avoid unnecessary interaction with those types of people. You may be at risk of losing more than you think.... Now with that said just let that sink in.

Going on vacation is an experience everyone should have. I highly endorse going on vacations. It gives you a chance to relax and enjoy life without everyday worries and problem. People who take vacations are more likely to be more productive and experience a higher self-esteem when compared to workaholics. Just being in a different environment gives you that mental break so that you can appreciate being alive. I am all for hard-work and dedication, but more than that I recommend a well deserved, nice vacation. Most workplaces only offer 1or 2 weeks a year but I believe ideally 3-4 weeks is sufficient. Take time for yourself and your family and use vacations to relax, unwind and create lasting fun memories. Like the saying goes "All work and no play make Jack a dull boy" …now with that said just let that sink in.

Positive thinking must be followed by actions. If you don't follow it up you are only a dreamer. The problem with being a dreamer is that you are stuck in the world of possibilities but no active way of getting out of the dream world. You have to get moving and attempt to bring your ideas to life. It is like buying a plane ticket to a destination but never showing up at the airport. Don't be stuck as a dreamer, but rather be a doer that way your vision can become a working reality ….now with that said just let that sink in.

If you are going to be successful and make progress in life you are going to have to learn to get along with people who are different from you. Different beliefs, religions, races, nationality etc. Successful people don't hold on to prejudices. Rather they accept people differences and prefer to see it as uniqueness. They know that not everyone is a duplicate of them thus resulting in different ideologies. When you go to your workplace, social event or place of worship go with the mentality that it is ok to be different. It would be a very boring world if we were all the same…. now with that said just let that sink in.

Low self-esteem is one of the most depressing situations one can experience. It can affect anybody at anytime. When an individual is in this state, it can bring about serious physical and mental health issues. Unfortunately a lot of people never make it out of that state. Low esteem will cause women to stay in abusive or demoralizing relationships, teens to drop out of school, people to always have a gloomy outlook on life and be caught up in the tornado of negativity. Today is a different day. Lift up your head and remember that you can beat this cycle. Become an active participant in your own life. Seek out positive influences (friends, family, TV shows, activities, and group/association) that encourage positive lifestyles. I know you have what it takes to overcome and win. Factor all these and pronounce your belief in God almighty and you will win the fight………..now with that said just let that sink in.

Never let anybody define who you are. Never let them tell you that you are not this, that or the other. No one has the right to define you or confine you. Don't let anyone clothe you with the fabric of negativity and the apparel of limitations. You are basically two things in life. Who God says you are and who you say you are. Drape yourself with the latest styles of confidence, positivity, self-esteem, faith, dedication, persistence and wear the crown of self–actualization. See the greatness inside of you…..with that said just let that sink in.

If you ever notice in all my writings, I focus on the individual. Why is that? I personally believe that we all have to work on ourselves before we can go out into the world and affect change. I always encourage self development, because if you produce a better you then you are more prepared to deal with life's challenges, scenarios and interactions with others. Your main concern in this life should always be getting yourself right and constantly improving your traits. You are a never ending work in progress…now with that said just let that sink in.

We have all made mistakes in life and nobody is perfect. Sometimes it is actions that we could have avoided and other times, it maybe involuntary. Whatever it is, I just want to tell you that it is time you forgive yourself. Feeling bad about mistakes is a normal human response, however wallowing in these feelings creates an atmosphere of depression, self-pity, low self esteem and a sorrowful mindset (none of which are good for you). You may have made a mistake but the best way to overcome it is to try to rectify it. Get up and look to make amends. Disappointments come along with mistakes but I am overly impressed with resiliency to recompense for the mistake. It's time you forgave yourself........now with that said just let that sink in

I will take on the role of being a judge and you will be the defendant. In my court, I won't be handing out prison sentences but I will only be handing out life sentences. Guess what I found you guilty on the charge of allowing negative thoughts/people/situations/actions to stop you from accomplishing your goals. I, Judge Kevon Husband, sentence you to a lifetime of positive thoughts/actions, meaningful friendships and loving interactions, blessings in your family/spiritual/financial life and boundless success. This sentence will run concurrently. However my sentences are not subject to appeal and there is no parole eligibility ....now with that said just let that sink in.

Derek Redman was an Olympic 400meters sprinter representing Great Britain in the 1992 Olympic games in Barcelona. One of the favorites for an Olympic medal he suffered a severe hamstring injury in the semi-final rounds and was eliminated. However tragic it may sound with all the pain he continued on hobbling and his father broke through security to help his son to the finish-line. The crowd there knew they were witnessing a man overcoming a physical barrier urged him on. That moment he became a legend in the eyes of the world for his determination and "never give up attitude". He ended up getting endorsement with Visa and was featured for years in their spirit of the Olympic commercials for years to come. He didn't win the race but he succeeded in inspiring millions across the world in that moment. Embrace the same spirit Mr. Redman had in 1992 and remember to never give up..........now with that said just let that sink in.

Father's Day is supposed to be a celebration of the men who have nurtured and protected the young people in our society. Unfortunately, a lot of biological fathers deny children and a lot of people grow up without the inspiration and protection of one.1 Timothy 5 verse 8 stated "but if anyone provides not for his own, and especially for those of his house, he has denied the faith and is worse than an infidel". Well we have a lot of infidels amongst us today. A lot of father's day cards will remain on the shelves of major retailers. We need more stand up men in society. The nation needs men to be the right kind of influence on our young people. Father's day is a day to celebrate all the men who have impacted and set a standard for excellence with their children. Not for the tax return daddies or the disappearing dads..........now with that said just let that sink in.

I believe everyone should hear the story of John and Randy Davis. They were diagnosed with muscular dystrophy at the respective ages of 2 and 5 which led to them being mostly wheelchair bound. They enrolled in Boy Scout program and there was an alternative curriculum for disabled. They both rejected the alternative program and signed up for the regular courses. Seven years later John achieved the highest rank of the Boys Scout Association, Eagle Scout and one year later Randy attained the rank. Today you might be reading this and have a physical disability. Don't use that as an excuse to settle or not to attempt to achieve your goals. All a disability says is that you can accomplish goals differently. Never allow your disability to define you…now with that said just let that sink in

Do you have critics? If you are a living breathing human being chances are you do. That is just a part of life. No matter what you do in this life whether it be done in excellence or an error is made there is always someone ready to criticize you. I got news for you. All the greats in history have had critics: Nelson Mandela, Winston Churchill, Charles Darwin, and Albert Einstein etc… They didn't allow that to define them but they ignored it and continued on their path to greatness. Today you too should continue on the path towards greatness and not be bothered but skeptics. Put it this way. Jesus had critics but who do you know more about? Jesus or his critics….now with that said just let that sink in.

I once heard a story about an athlete with a lot of potential and he specialized in the hurdle events. One time he qualified for a tournament and the prize for the winner on the event would be a brand new car. So as the competitors lined up he got a look at the vehicle and he was determined to make it his own. So as the race began in its early stages he began to build a substantial lead. Midway in the race his lead began to build even further. At about the ¾ way mark he took a glance at the car, lost concentration and collided with a hurdle and fell to the floor. He eventually got back up but he was only able to finish in 3rd place. We must focus on the immediate goals ahead of us and not be easily distracted. Not only should we keep our eyes on the prize but make sure it is the right one….now with that said just let that sink in.

The word "Philanthropy" is used a lot when wealthy people donate money to human/social causes. I decided to research its meaning and I found out it was originally a Greek term. It is actually two words. "Philos" meaning love and "anthropos" meaning man/human being. Literally it implies love for mankind/human being. Christ himself commanded us to "love your neighbor as yourself" (Mark 12.31). So let's display love to our fellow man. One does not need to be financial wealthy to be a Philanthropist. All that is needed is a willing heart and spirit full of love. Sharing encouraging words with someone going through a tough time, volunteering at a soup kitchen, helping a child with their homework, offering that neighbor a lift when driving past them. We all have the ability everyday to be a philanthropist…now with that said just let that sink in.

I don't take writing these positive affirmations lightly. I honestly believe it is a gift given by God to encourage people. I don't do it for likes on social media. I don't do it to make myself look good or give myself the appearance of being knowledgeable. I am writing them because I know that every day we fight battles and whatever positive inspirations we can see might just be what we need. I try to do my part in helping to keep people encouraged. When I write I will honestly tell you that it's God's direction. Yes, I may be quite intelligent but these writings are beyond my wisdom and I am not ashamed to say that God puts it on my heart. So if what I write inspires you and gets you over the finish line, I can't take any credit. God is the author I'm just the one who does the typing….now with that said just let that sink in.

One of my favorite all-time Television shows is from the mid 1980's named MacGyver. Thirty years plus after, it still sends chills in my body when I watch it. It is always intriguing to see when the lead character (MacGyver) is stuck in an unbecoming situation, immediately uses his wits, knowledge of the sciences and whatever resources available to conjure a way out of the situation. Let's take after MacGyver and use the resources we have at our disposal to develop ourselves and achieve the desired results. Stop looking at what we don't have and start making use of our skills. This was a real nostalgic moment for me and I hope you learned from it…now with that said just let that sink in.

One of the things I love is when people get rewarded and experience success. I experience an extreme sense of delight when I see people get promotions, salary hikes, graduate from school at any level, get that dream job/career etc… You never know what someone might have been going through and that breakthrough might just be what they needed. I love seeing the rewards of hard work and dedication in others lives. Delighting in the success of others shows that you have the right intentions in your heart towards them and that you are thinking in a positive manner. Some people get jealous when others succeed and express resentment. Don't allow yourself to get those feelings…. That is called Hate. Don't be a hater but rather let it spur you on to achieve your own successes……..now with that said just let that sink in.

I have never liked the term "third world country". Not just for Geo-Socio-economic reasons but because it put the idea into people minds that depending on where you were born it makes you better than someone else. I wholeheartedly look at this term as derogatory because it cheapens the value of the life of the populations in those nations that are referred to by this term. Besides, most of the world's wealth is actually found in these nations. Everyone regardless of geographic location or nationality is special. No one deserves better treatment than someone else. We need to rid ourselves of the mentality that a place of birth determines how we see others. Now if only we can discourage our leaders to refrain from such terms……. now with that said just let that sink in.

I am of the utmost belief that most people in life get stuck in a rut because we aim too low; in the same breath I believe that we all have the potential for greatness but unfortunately we don't act and think like it. Some people are afraid to aim too high so they set the bar at an average expectation. The end result tends to be an unsatisfying life. I therefore urge you to have some confidence in yourself and set grandiose goals and work to accomplish them. Hebrews 10 verse 35-36 states "Therefore do not throw away your confidence, which has a great reward. For you have need of endurance, so that when you have done the will of God you may receive what is promised." With God's help and your desire to be successful you will accomplish your goals …..Now with that said just let that sink in

Let me familiarize you with a term called the "Positive Movement Gas Pedal" coined by a fellow named Jeffrey Allen. Pretty much the term means keep on moving with positivity. Always seek out the positive. Put yourself in a position in which you are well placed for positive outcomes

/interactions /scenarios /opportunities. When a car is in motion and a pothole is ahead, the driver most of the time avoids the pothole. He doesn't turn around and quit driving but instead he keeps moving. Same away when facing with negative scenarios we must continue forward with our positive course of action. Thanks Jeff for giving us this term. Now with that said just let that sink in.

Let me brief you on a financial issue which affects us all. Many of us struggle when it comes to this particular topic. Saving. It is a really hard thing to do especially in today's economic climate. All the emphasis is on spending and shopping and not enough on saving. After all it is easier to spend than to save. I have a simple solution that is pretty basic. Every pay period have your bank automatically put aside a set amount of money (let's say $20) from your earnings in a savings account. That way the money is never missed and you won't get a chance to spend that money. Proverbs 10:4 states "A slack hand causes poverty, but the hand of the diligent makes rich." and Proverbs 13:11 "Wealth gained hastily will dwindle, but whoever gathers little by little will increase it." A person who saves in his present is actually investing in his future…now with that said just let that sink in

There is a common expression people like to use especially when they are doing wrong and they are told about it. They adopt a defensive counter and say "you're not God you can't judge. Let me clarify the difference between judging someone and correcting someone. Judging occurs when people usually have some sort of pre-misguided notion and can involve malice or prejudice. Correction is when you pretty much call it as it is. If I see someone stealing and I tell them about it that is correction. It is sad that a lot of people refuse correction and often view it as judging. However, it is also sad when people have pre-conceived thoughts and judge others. It is important that we know and learn the difference when applying it to our lives….now with that said just let that sink in

One day I met one of my colleagues in the store and I greeted her with a joke and she was not too responsive to it. So I asked if she was ok and she told me that she was not a morning person. What is a morning person? Or an evening person? I believe that people use those terms for an excuse because of a bad mood. Don't allow your mood to be determined by the time of day but rather from the time you wake up look forward to a day filled with positive vibes and optimism. Just so you know every day you open your eyes is a good day. If you don't believe me just try missing one of them…now with that said just let that sink in

There are three words I will always advise anyone to make part of their lifestyle. Love, live and Impact. Love people and have a genuine heart. In the bible Mark 12.31 Christ commands us to "love your neighbor as yourself" show love and you will receive also. Live and appreciate all the experiences both good and bad because experiences foster wisdom. James 1:2-3 "Count it all joy, when you meet trials of various kinds because you know the testing of your faith produces various perseverance." Finally, have a positive impact on the people you meet... Don't allow others negativity to corrupt you. 1 Corinthians 15:33 "Don't be deceived, bad company ruins good moral. Now go out there Love, Live and Impact the world...now with that said just let that sink in

Did someone hurt you in the past and it is affecting you in the present? Hear this...The people that hurt you don't go around talking about it so why should you. I know it wasn't nice and it's not easy but move on with your life. When you constantly live in the past you are actually wasting all your emotional energy which can be used to better your future and foster new meaningful relationships. Whether it happened in 1995, 1978 or recently I want to urge you to leave the past in the past. It is not easy, but I believe that you can. The optimist looks forward to life opportunities and not back at life's misfortunes and bad experiences.... now with that said just let that sink in

It was in 2006 I decided to consciously live a positive life but what I didn't know is that it would take me over 8 years for it to manifest in my habits. Determination is what got me there. I had to learn to speak positive, think positive, eat positive etc... How to handle situations beyond my sphere of influence, how to shut up/listen and humble myself. How to get up and go and stop making excuses or waiting for stuff to happen. How to let other people get the last word when I know they are completely wrong and how to read positive books to add to my knowledge. How to control my emotions, how to learn proper time management, how to avoid getting to the point of obscene language and how to get to that point of self control. I thank God for all my experiences and his grace to get me to that point. I share this so you know that it took a lot of work to get me to this point. Same way I advise you to work on yourself. Now with that said just let that sink in

Today is a good day. You are alive, you are healthy and you are blessed. Even if things are not at a zenith level in your life, you are in a pretty good spot. Things could be a lot worst. Stop looking at everyone else and learn to appreciate the good you have going for you in your life. ….. Now with that said just let that sink in

Be encouraged, keep up the good work. You have come a long way. You might not get credit from the people around you however, it is important that you don't use that as an excuse to revert to the old you. Whether it be you trying to be a better parent to your kids or cutting down on the number of cigarettes you smoke remember Rome was not built in day. Never get boastful. Humbly acknowledge God for your progress and continue climbing your ladder of self development. ... Now with that said just let that sink in

There is a huge misconception circulating in society and a lot of people are blind to it but they subscribe to the concept. People have the notion that if you disagree with a certain lifestyle or belief you must either hate or fear such. Listen you don't have to believe what someone else believes to love and respect them. The same way they are entitled to have their belief you are also entitled to have your own. You don't have to compromise your beliefs to be compassionate. We should all be mature enough to understand that disagreement doesn't equate to hate...now with that said just let that sink in

The two strongest words in the English language both just happen to be four letter words. They also are the complete opposite actions and emotions of each other. Those words are love and hate. They will both control and consume a person's reaction, emotions and interactions with others. Also they are both impossible to feel concurrently. It will either be one or the other. I say this as a reminder to us as we are creatures of emotions and actions which lead us to develop habits. Be careful in your expression of these traits......now with that said just let that sink in

Most of us live in the free world...at least physically. However many of us are still trapped in the cycle of emotional/social incarceration. Worried about how others perceive us to be. This has lead to the creation of a whole new demographic which I call "people pleasers". Living to impress others, afraid to be one's self because you will be mocked and conform to unnecessary social standards. Similar to peer pressure but it affects a wider range of the population. Today I want to encourage you to walk to the tune of your own beat. Don't be afraid to be different. Those people who think different change the world or let's say their own lives have ventured on the path less trodden. Being a people pleaser only limits your own ambitions and devalues your character. Think with your own mind and liberate your mind for emotional/social incarceration.... Now with that said just let that sink in

I always say this. I can't believe anything for anyone and I cannot disbelieve anything for anyone. What matters to me is what I believe for myself, what someone thinks about my belief is none of my business. I'm not concerned with such. External opinions didn't originate from within me so why should I allow it to become part of the fabric of my belief. The same should apply to you. To paraphrase international renowned motivation speaker Les brown "Don't let someone's expectation of you become your reality" ...with that said just let that sink in

Let me give you the tale of two security guards I was observing sometime ago. The first guard had a mean demeanor, didn't say good morning to the tenants of the building he was stationed at, yell and screamed at everyone he didn't like. The second security guard had a much more pleasant demeanor. He greeted everyone with a joyous greeting, had delightful interaction with the tenants and often displayed a sense of pride on the job. I spoke to the second guard and he told me "whether I have a good or bad day I shouldn't take it out on anybody. Besides being mean doesn't make my job any easier" Guess who is in line for a promotion? Your attitude always effect how far you can rise in life...........now with that said, just let that sink in

The great English playwright William Shakespeare once said "All the world's a stage, and all the men and women merely players; they have their exits and their entrances". No one is irreplaceable in your life. Never allow people to stay longer in your life than necessary. Don't keep people in your life who you know are not good for you. Lose negative people and embrace the positive ones. This is your life and you have the authority as to who you allow into your circle....... now with that said just let that sink in

When you work hard and are very diligent you won't look for shortcuts to success. I once read in what I believe is the greatest self help book ever written "See you at the top" by Zig ziglar - "there is no elevator to success; you are going to have to take the stairs." You have the ability all you need to do is to work hard and be consistent with it. I'm not a statistician but I can almost guarantee every time you attempt a shortcut method for success your failure rate will be 100%. ...now with that said just let that sink in.

When they laugh at you don't feel bad. When they mock and belittle you don't spend time worrying about it. When they perceive you and try to convince everyone that you are something you are not remember this.... They are jealous. They always want to see you beneath them and never make any progress. What they think about you and how they perceive you has nothing to do with you. That's on them. As long as you know in your heart you have stayed true to your character and are honest and true to yourself you will be okay. Let God deal with the haters. Sometimes I disappoint myself but then I remember I have to pick myself up. I am human and I have made mistakes and I am not infallible. I have great days and I have not so great days. However I try to make the most of my great days so that when the not so great days surface I have enough from the great days to keep me going. Tell yourself these words anytime you feel down ....now with that said just let that sink in.

Remember when we were young and believed that what we wanted to be when we grow up was possible. Remember the child-like mindset that made the impossible seemed possible? What happened? I will tell you. Negative words/ thoughts/ actions came upon us. We started listening to all the cannots, would nots and should nots from those around us. Self confidence was gradually replaced by self doubt and an acceptance of mediocrity thus leading us to stop pursuing our goals. I encourage you to turn back the clock on your adult self to the child-like mentality and believe in your dreams. Remember every dream and goal has a chance once you believe it is possible. Ignore the negative broadcasts in your atmosphere. No one can kill your dreams. Your dream only dies when you allow it. Now what that said just let that sink in.

Be that type of person who dislikes negativity. If you are in a room and the atmosphere is negative you will be uncomfortable to be surrounded by such. If you are a positive individual, don't make excuses to be around it. That would be like being an in boat which is taking in water and saying "well at least it is not on my end of the boat". Certainly, you will get wet soon. Same way it is with negativity. If the basement is flooded do you stay and drown or do you seek higher ground. Rise above negativity every opportunity you get…That is the best decision you will ever make…Now with that said just let that sink in

You are the first person who will exert influence on your kids. Quick story when my son was born I looked into his beautiful bright eyes and told the nurses to take a selfie with him because this is the future president of the United Stated of America. Right from the moment of birth I began to speak positive things into his life. Up to this day I refer to my son as Mr. President. I don't focus on what he can't do, I just tell him that he can and he will. Speaking the right things into our children puts them on the path for greatness. Nobody should discourage or limit their kids. Teach them that the sky is the limit unless of course you're telling them to be an astronaut...haha... Now with that said just let that sink in

Something I realized about myself when I was grow ing up is that I was always different. My friends would like one brand and I would be the only person to like another. When some people would want to go left I would always go right. My particular taste was always varied from the mainstream. I mentioned this about myself to say never be afraid to be different. Conformity kills your individual character especially when it is something you know is not for you. God made us all different and unique and we should embrace Mona Lisa doesn't go around trying to be a Picasso painting.... Now with that said just let that sink in

If you think you can you will and if you think you can't you won't. It is all mental. If you put in the time and dedication to whatever you are trying to accomplish but your mind is not right you won't achieve it. However if mindset, purpose and dedication are all on the positive side of the tracks the results will be in your favor….. Now with that said just let that sink in

A little piece of advice. Stay away from the people who always complain and find some negative about every situation. If you don't then they will eventually contaminate your thinking and you will by defacto become a victim of what Zig Ziglar calls "Stinking thinking". Every opportunity to complain, whine and express discontent is what you should avoid. Instead get your body and mind away from that atmosphere and become the person who sees the problem as an opportunity to create or find a solution….. now with that said just let that sink in

I will use coffee beans to illustrate something positive for all of us. When they are placed in extremely hot water they don't succumb to the heat but rather they change the physical and chemical makeup of the liquid to what we drink as coffee. It didn't allow the pressure and heat to get to it but rather it changed its environment. Don't allow your environment to influence you but rather you are the one to lay down a path of influence. Don't allow life pressures to get to you. Be innovative and you will soon see your respective situations transform to greatness……… now with that said just let that sink in

Germany is a central European nation of great economic power and one of the most progressive countries in the world. However, Germany has a tainted past due to the antics of Adolf Hilter: A lot of atrocities, war-crimes, genocide and racism plagued Germany under his rule. The Government of Germany ashamed by the actions of the past put into place a system which actively denounces racism and seeks to amend its past by embracing people of all nations to work, study and live in the country. Germany doesn't live in its past but rather it focuses on how it can be a better country for all that call it home. If you had a horrific incident in your past, try to focus on making the future better. Follow the example of Deutschland (Germany)…now with that said just let that sink in

One thing I have never been ashamed to say is that all my life I have always been different. I am extremely proud of it. Being different, thinking different and living different provides a platform for us to express our originality. Our differences are what make us unique. Never be ashamed to be different…now with that said just let that sink in

I salute everyone who is still fighting the good fight. You have been through the toughest situations and you are still standing. That shows me you have grit, determination and a never give up attitude. Your character is one which I admire and I just want you to know people like you inspire people like me. I know you're emotionally, physically, spiritually drained but somehow you keep on going. Every day you wake up, show up and don't complain. So whether it be Fighting cancer, struggling to take care of your kids by working 2 jobs, walking away from that abusive relationship or in pursuit of your GED while being a single parent you have put rubber to the road and deserve credit for such. All of you are my heroes….now with that said just let that sink in

Everyone has an important role to play in society. One job I am most appreciative of is the sanitation workers aka garbage men. A lot of people look down at the profession but they are some of the most needed services in most nations. Without them and their services we would be at constant risk for many diseases and plagues such as cholera, typhoid fever, and leptospirosis. I see the importance and relevance in their work. Same way I suggest that you see the importance in everyone's work. Don't look down at occupations but rather acknowledge its significance towards the maintenance of our society…… now with that said just let that sink in

The Mexican national soccer team is one of the world's more formidable teams. When playing at home in their almighty Azteca stadium all the odds are in their favor. High altitudes and one of the world's most intimidating crowds (95000) they always have the opposition teams at a mental disadvantage. This physical and psychological advantage compounded by the fact that they never lost a world cup qualifying game at home… that was until in 2001 a very determined Costa Rican national team would upset them at home by a final score of 2-1. How was Costa Rica able to do the undoable? Determination, Grit and adopting a giant slaying mentality. Self belief and hard work are keys to everyone's success. Stop looking at the size of the giant and start believing in your abilities to overcome the giants in your life…. now with that said just let that sink in

One of the most important things we can do in life is ask questions. This is one of the primary/ simplest ways we will acquire knowledge. In my life up to this day I always ask questions. I also always try to answer any question. There are no stupid questions. I would rather repeat an answer for a question than rather have someone not ask a question because they think it is stupid. Some people laugh at the questions of others which I believe is a counterproductive behavior. If you don't know how else will you find out? Going forward I want us to remember this…It is better to ask a so called "stupid question" and get an answer than to pretend to know the answer and display yourself as a chalartan….. Now with that said just let that sink in

The blame game stops here. You are responsible for where you are at in life. Whether you are successful or not at the end of the day you are the person in charge of your life. We all made decisions based on whatever it was.

Circumstances and curveballs are constants in life so to use them as excuses is unacceptable. A famous writer and speaker named Earl Nightingale once said "We are all self made, but only the successful will admit it". When I drive in my vehicle the road is rarely smooth or without traffic but yet still I get to my destination. The same applies to your life, your goals and aspirations. now with that said just let that sink in

I hardly ever write about relationships and I have just cause. The purpose behind my writings is to encourage the individuals to develop themselves (character traits/personality/mentality). The reason for this is because how are you going to deal with someone else and you haven't gotten a solid foundation for you to stand. Constant self development is a key in everyone's life. Focus on becoming a better you before you insert yourself into a relationship. That is your responsibility to yourself... now with that said just let that sink in

I met a gentleman named Mr. Arnold Francis and while he was not at the zenith of his life financially he was definitely a poster boy for positivity. We spoke about the negatives in society and he told me his desire was to turn the negatives into positives. He eventually designed his own jerseys which took traditionally negative/derogatory slangs into positive and uplifting acronyms. While he may have gotten some flack about it, he has demonstrated his willingness to rise above negativity regardless of opinions. We can learn from his example. Turn the negatives in our respective lives into positives and not worry about the critics............now with that said just let that sink in

Sometimes when playing a video game you get stuck on different levels and it is quite frustrating. Trust me I know. To past that particular obstacle/level it sometimes might take hours, days, weeks, months and in extreme cases years. However, once you finally overcome that level you are able to advance in the game and experience a sense of euphoria. The same way it is with our lives. Once we get up and actively work at our personal herculean task regardless of how long it takes when we overcome it, we will experience the same sense of euphoria with the accomplishment. Keep on working at whatever it is you are trying to accomplish... now with that said just let that sink in

I always say to people if you say you can you will and if you say you can't then you won't. Proverbs 18.21 states "The tongue has the power of life and death." Whatever you pronounce out of your mouth is what you will decree in your life. Guard your words. Use them to create a positive platform for your success rather than speak your demise... now with that said just let that sink in

I am a believer in thinking outside the box. Expanding the realm of thinking. Finding ways and means instead of finding excuses. We have been taught to always fit the mold that is set for us by our parents, schools, religious groups, organizations and society. Anyone can meet the status quo but the highly successful people make their own mold. Instead of looking at pros and cons I invite you to start a new trend of looking at the pros and working on accomplishing them. If we think positive we can only breed positivity…….. Now with that said just let that sink in

Everyone has a moral and social responsibility as a human being to speak out against the wrongs in our society. It doesn't matter if it personally affects you or not, when we all turn a blind eye that is all that is needed for evil deeds to continue. I saw this quote about 15years ago and it reminded me why we have a responsibility to say something *"First they came for the Socialists, and I did not speak out—because I was not a Socialist. Then they came for the Trade Unionists, and I did not speak out— because I was not a Trade Unionist. Then they came for the Jews, and I did not speak out— because I was not a Jew. Then they came for me—and there was no one left to speak for me.* (**Martin Niemöller).** Think about that. ….now with that said just let that sink in

I look back at my life and then I see all the people who have hurt me with words, actions and deeds. People who treated me like I was trash, People who lied, People who had the world of negative things to say about me. I said to myself I forgive them. Why did I do that? Because what I have learned is that forgiveness is for me and not necessary the other person. The best part about forgiving someone is that you are able to start the process of moving on with your life. You don't necessarily have to associate with them but with action of forgiveness the emotional burden is lifted off your shoulders. As C.S Lewis said "There are far, far better things ahead than any we leave behind"…. now with that said just let that sink in

Everyone who associates with me knows at least these two things about me, I love to be positive and I love to laugh/ smile. I don't necessarily try to be the life of the party but I appreciate an atmosphere filled with happiness and laughter. I like to do my best to impact those around me into a healthy environment where we can be surrounded with humor. Sometimes I even laugh at myself. Keep yourself smiling and wherever you go ride abreast with happiness. Bring happiness with you everywhere….now with that said just let that sink in

Tell yourself you will not live with grudges. Stop looking back at what was and look at your future with optimism. If your mindset is always in reverse you won't ever go forward. We can't change the past but we can make our future what we want. As Doc Brown from the movie "Back To The Future" said … "The future has finally arrived," Yes, it is different than we all thought. But don't worry

— it just means your future hasn't been written yet. No one's has. Your future is whatever you make it, so make it a good one."....now with that said just let that sink in.

At times we may lack the self confidence to believe in ourselves. Sometimes we may not emotionally have the ability to push forward to achieve our goals. At times like these, we need people who believe in us, who believe we can accomplish our goals. I once had Pastor Renny Clarke tell me these words. "There are levels to you that the world has never seen but it is up to you to decide if you allow the world to see it". Hence I always say surround yourself with positive uplifting people - people who see the goodness in you and refuse to allow you to express unbelief in your abilities..... Now with that said just let that sink in

A big social problem in society is that we are afraid to say what we believe because we are worried about offending other people who may have a different belief. Stop worrying about offending others. Regardless of what you do, you will always offend someone so I highly suggest you feel free to express your beliefs just as long as you do so in a respectable manner............now with that said just let that sink in

The most successful people are the ones who do the most uncomfortable tasks. Get comfortable with the uncomfortable. Do things that you won't regularly do in order to get the results you desire. 100 percent of the people who refuse to do the extra work needed to be successful usually aren't. What is it you desire? Invest your nights and days with blood, sweat and tears to be successful. Push yourself extra. When you are tired all that means is that you are tired, it doesn't mean you don't have anything left in the tank. No one has ever ran a marathon and won without a lot of sweat….now with that said just let that sink in

Racism is a taught behavior passed down like culture. Nobody was ever born with the concept of race. Racism is a factor of hate and fear manufactured by ignorance. The sad part is that a lot of people have racist attributes and don't even know it. Being the optimist, I offer a futuristic solution. Start teaching your children the attributes of love, respect, tolerance and appreciation of mankind. The glasses of racism are not stationary but removable. A great man once said; love your neighbor as yourself. ...... Now with that said just let that sink in

I have always been a believer of working in silence and letting my success speak for itself. Just as a general rule, I don't tell people what I am going to …I just do it. We don't need to announce everything to everyone. Be the type of person that allows their success to surprise people. You should be so focused on your goals that you have no time to worry about broadcasting to others. You don't need to speak for your success but rather your success should speak for you....now with that said just let that sink in

Here is a simple task. Take a pen and get a dictionary and cross out the following words: Can't, wouldn't, shouldn't and impossible. By eliminating these words from your vocabulary you will also abandon them from your thinking. Say positive words which will lead to positive actions, results and lifestyles, .now with that said just let that sink in

When I was in college I had a ton of people I would associate with but as I got older I realized I had to make some adjustments in my friendships and associations with others. Now I have a much smaller circle of friends but the individuals in that circle possess similar goals and understand the power of positivity. In life we all have to recognize what we desire from our interactions with others. We all go through changes and not everyone fits into our mold throughout our lives. If you are a positive person you have got to learn to let go of that high school buddy who is engaging in activities counterproductive to your ambitions. Forget about having a ton of friends but rather focus on having relationships based on quality interactions.........now with that said just let that sink in

I will say this once. Not because someone doesn't believe what you believe doesn't make you any better than them or makes you right and they wrong. Whether it be politics, history, religion or simple common views everyone is entitled to have their own perspective. We have no right to condemn anyone because of the way they see the world is different from us. Focus on what you believe and stop wasting time trying to convince others away from what they believe. Smart people know that everyone will never agree on everything.....now with that said just let that sink in

Let's talk about two F words. Faith and fear. Faith is a belief that a result is capable, possible or attainable regardless of circumstances. Fear is also a belief that a desired result won't be attained because there is something that will occur to stop such. Too many of us live with the concept of fear instead of faith. Faith sees the finish line and the glory. Fear sees the disappointment and downward spiral. Today I encourage you to live your life in faith and never in fear. Fear has a much lower success rate than faith..... Now with that said just let that sink in

I was once asked why I'm so positive. Don't I see all the bad stuff and live in the same world as everyone else? Do I live in an alternative reality? This was my response... I see what goes on in the world both good and bad but my perspective is to focus on the positives rather than the negatives of life. Positive thinking leads to positive an action which in turn leads to us doing something about our lives therefore giving us the belief that we can take control of our destiny. To quote Zig Ziglar the man I consider to be the greatest motivational speaker ever "Positive thinking won't help you do anything but it will help you do everything better than negative thinking will." We already know about the negatives, try seeking out the positives in life. It is a starting point for change and greatness...now with that said just let that sink in

If you choose to focus on what is wrong in society that is your choice. I want to be the individual whose energies are directed towards a high level. I want to focus on the positives in life rather than the negatives. Society has engineered us to embrace the negative or even find a negative in a positive. Colossians 3:2 states "Set your affections on the things above, not on the things on the earth." My positivity comes from my heavenly father that is why I am not fazed by all the mainstream and social media negativity. If people think I am too optimistic it is because they cannot see what I see. ...... Now with that said just let that sink in

Negative people only see in the short term. They suffer from the here and now syndrome. They base their future on the present. Positive folks however, plan their future in the present and understand that your current situation doesn't determine your future. Only you can chart your future by your actions in the present. Be a visionary and work towards the life you desire. Don't just take opportunity but also create opportunity. As the old saying goes "God helps those who help themselves" ...... now with that said just let that sink in

If you want to live a positive life you have to get rid of a negative mindset. No accomplishment has ever come from a negative thought. Your thought process is reflected in every aspect of your life. Never get accustom to thinking negative. Every success started from a positive mindset. Today I encourage you to make your mind a factory of positive thoughts. Remember negative thoughts lead to negative actions and have never gotten anyone the results they wanted in life........ Now with that said just let that sink in

If you are waiting on the future to improve your life then your life will never be improved. If you waiting on something to happen before you start, chances are you won't ever get started. What if that thing you are waiting on never happens? You can only lay the path for your future by allocating your time and resources today. A car has the potential to carry you anywhere but if the gear is in park you will get nowhere. Your situation will not change unless you take steps to change it in the present.....now with that said just let that sink in

I always tell people the same thing I tell myself. Focus on the task at hand and don't be distracted by current, irrelevant affairs. We tend to get easily distracted and sometimes get caught up in the whole atmosphere of nothingness that we forget our goals in life. Focus on you, focus on developing yourself. Don't let the media, politicians or society make you forget your purpose. John 17 verses 15-16 "I do not ask you to take them out of the world, but to keep them from the evil one." They are not of the world, even as I am not of the world. ..... Now with that said just let that sink in

Tell yourself it is possible. You lived your entire life with conditioned negativity – in a lot of cases from parents/ family, teachers, friends, haters, coaches and even religious leaders. Today that cycle stops. Stop allowing the negative to stop you from trying. I once heard a story of the frog that was climbing a tree and all the other frogs were telling him to come back down because there was a frog-eating bird at the top of tree. However, the frog was deaf and he thought they were cheering him on. Long story short. He got to the top of the tree and ate the bird. Today is the day you develop conditioned positivity. Be like that frog and be deaf to the naysaying. Today you have a new belief -anything is possible. Now with that said just let that sink in

Your friends are a reflection of you. People with similar ambitions will always be found in similar circles. As an example, eagles soar high up in the sky but chickens spend most of the time looking at the ground. Eagles and chickens don't socialize. Your ambitions will always match your associates /friendships/ relationships. There is a Japanese saying which goes like this "When the character of a man is not clear to you. Look at his friends". Also I saw another saying which goes "show me your friends and I will show you your future"….now with that said just let that sink in

Everyone claims to want a grand chance or opportunity to do something great but many people when presented with opportunity take it for granted. When you do nothing you will get nothing. 0+0 is always 0. Every success started with taking a small opportunity. Today be that person who jumps at the positive opportunity to create your own success. Remember every house started with lying of one brick….. Now with that said just let that sink in

This is a sad and unwavering truth. Until a person is ready to believe in themself no one and I mean no one will be able to convince them of their ability to achieve success. Many people lose the battle in their head and until they break that kind of unbelief within themselves everything they attempt will be destined to fail. Don't be that type of individual. Never strike yourself with the nightstick of negativity but instead be open to the fact that every successful person started with a positive belief...now with that said just let that sink in

Sometime ago I was in the gas station and a man approached me and offered to pump my gas for free. So I was like I guess it was not a problem so I said ok. While pumping the gas I asked him why is he doing this and he said that he recently lost his job and he is just trying to be kind because he believes kindness is the way to go. Afterwards when he was finished I offered him the last $5 I had. Initially he refused but I insisted so he accepted and started to cry. I gave him a hug even though he did not have the best of appearance and sent him on his way. Point being never look down on anybody. Matthew 25 verse 40 states" Verily I say unto you, Inasmuch as ye have done it unto one of the least of these my brethren, ye have done it unto me." Regardless of situation of appearance treat people well. Now with that said just let that sink in

This is how I live my life. I focus on the positive, focus on the good and I do my best to encourage others and not to criticize. People may not like how I think. People may not like what I say. People may not like what I believe. It is none of my business what they say, think or believe about me. It is absolutely irrelevant to my cause. This is the way I live my life. Positivity is my desire and personality. My goal is greatness not pleasing others..... Now with that said just let that sink in

Greatness has a lot in common with location. People who prefer mediocre lives usually stay within a certain square mileage. They only see the world as they know it maybe a couple of blocks or one neighborhood or so. The desire to be great will carry you to the path less trodden. Shooting stars stray from home. The desire to be great will cause you to go places, take the job opportunities others wouldn't and of course be called crazy. Believe me I have no problem being called crazy because as I once heard it said "to be great you have to be crazy". Today I encourage you denounce your rights to a common person and live a basic life and swear allegiance to the great person you are destined to be.......now with that said just let that sink in

I will tell you this; Salesmen/women are some of the most optimistic people in the world. They get told no so many times but yet still continue to keep on trying to make a sale. Sometimes I think they have no's for breakfast. They will take hundreds of no's undeterred just to get that one yes. The same way in life we should be undeterred when we get told no. To be successful you can't let no's discourage you from your desired outcome. To the optimistic person No means "Next Opportunity"….. Now with that said just let that sink in

Eagles are the apex predators of the sky. Armed with razor sharp talons, one of the keenest eyesight's of any animal, a strong muscular built and a beak which tears flesh easier than most knives, it is not hard to see why they are one of the birds at the top of the food chain. When they spot potential prey they pounce on the opportunity to obtain a meal. The Vulture however waits on other animals to make a kill before they can pounce on the opportunity not that they're incapable of hunting as they can be formidable predators but they wait for things to come their way. Which animal you think gets the prime choice of flesh from the kill. The Eagle of course. My point being when you create your own opportunities you will have better options but if you wait for opportunities and do nothing the options may not be as glorious ….. Now with that said just let that sink in

I personally believe that a key attribute to being successful is having patience. This trait has been fundamental in those in pursuit of greatness. However, we live in a world where people prefer to take the shortcuts & overnight schemes to achieve success. The problem with that is nothing in its natural order ever occurs in such a manner. For example let's use your current age. You weren't born that age but gradually you became that age because time had passed (days, weeks, month, and years). It took a natural progression to get there. You couldn't rush your age to be older so why would you rush anything in life? Impatient person seldom accomplishes anything in life however; the one who has patience in abundance will be one to keep on going until the desired result is achieved…. now with that said just let that sink in

You have spent a lifetime believing that you won't be successful. You have believed that everything bad happens to you. You have had circumstances and situations compound these beliefs into you method of thinking? Question - What have you done to influence or change the course of your life? Your life is like a car and you are the driver. It is up to you to chart you own path. If you walk down the same street you will always have the same view.....now with that said just let that sink in

African rhinos are some of the most aggressive animals in the world. Most animals in the wild do their best to avoid them...except the africanoxpecker. Strangely enough these two animals developed a mutually beneficial relationship where the oxpecker cleans the rhino's hide by eating the parasites therein also because the rhino has poor eyesight the oxpecker can warn it of potential danger approaching. The rhino provides a source of food and unintentionally protects the oxpecker from larger birds of prey. In doing my research I found out this type of relationship in the animal kingdom is called symbiosis. The relationship is mutually beneficial. Same way it should be with our relationships/friendships in life. We should always bring something to the table with our interaction with those around us. Life interactions should always be a give and take. The best relationships in life consist of mutual benefit.....now with that said just let that sink in

It is a tragedy that we get up every day go to work at jobs we don't like, give employers 100% but when it comes to our dreams and goals we are extremely passive. If we put that same energy into ourselves just imagine what your life could be like. You might actually be successful if you give some effort towards what you desire. I always tell people when you are not working on your dreams you are defacto helping someone else with their dream. It is time you kick start your desires in to overdrive. Have a goal, come up with a plan and learn what it will require, identify people and resources which can help you reach your goal. You already have the work ethic, now it's time you use it to your advantage ..... Now with that said just let that sink in

You ever notice weeds don't require any special treatment to grow. They will grow on good soil, bad soil and even through the cracks in concrete. They don't need much effort. Same way it is with negative thinking. Not much is required to be negative. However just like plants require good soil and maintenance, positive thinking requires some effort to be manifested into reality. In our daily lives we are confronted by negative thinking, just as weed killer eliminates the weeds, so we must extinguish negative thinking by reinforcing positive thinking. Weeds left alone to grow will destroy any garden, same way negative thinking will destroy your mind…..……….. Now with that said just let that sink in

The fundamental difference between an opportunist and a complainer is long term vision. The opportunist sees a scenario or problem and begins to look ahead and plan solutions. The complainer sees the exact scenario/problem accepts it for what it is and makes no attempt to alter it. Complainers contribute nothing to society and often are forgotten however, the opportunist are the ones who leave their mark on their sphere of influence - their family, community, workplace, nation and the globe. Today be the opportunist you were meant to be. Anyone can be a complainer…..now with that said just let that sink in

Many people want success but want it at a mediocre effort. The problem with that is success has absolutely nothing in common with mediocrity. To get the results you want in life, if you desire success, you have to do the things others will not. The people who say they won't to this or think some task is beneath them are those who are stuck in the same position and will be there for a while because of their level of thinking. The successful individual will do the tasks that seemingly are undesirable but worth it because they see the finish line. What is it you are trying to accomplish? What are you willing to do to obtain your goals? My friends the ball is in your court … now with that said just let that sink in

I heard of a quite interesting story about the Chinese bamboo which I believe we can all learn a lesson from. When the seed is planted it must be watered every day. If the seed goes a day without water it will die. This watering must continue everyday for 3 years. Within those 3 years the seed does not break the soil. After that time it breaks the soil and within 2 weeks it grows 90 feet. Question which period do you think was more important for the bamboo 3 years under the soils or the 2 weeks? The answer is the 3 years. Same way we need to plant the seeds in our life to accomplish our goals. All the hard work will not be in vain once you are true and stick with it every day. Eventually you will reach you goal and just like that Chinese bamboo your growth will be extraordinary. Stick at it and never give up ………….. now with that said just let that sink in

Why not you? Why not have your own success story? News flash everyday you live your life you are writing you own story. It is great to have the stories that inspire us but I think the greatest compliment we can get is when our life stories inspire others to greatness. Regardless of how much money you make or how much education you attain only the way we live our life matters most. Your life is your legacy to your friends, family and hopefully the world. I believe that your legacy is going to be one of success, glory and positivity…….. Now with that said just let that sink in

Make up your mind that no matter what comes your way you are going to make it. Nothing will stop you. Disappointments, negativity and circumstances are all just scenarios to overcome on your way to success. The honest truth is to be truly successful you have to be able to take life's punches and still keep on going. I know this from my own personal experiences. Life throws everything at you but yet you are still alive and reading this. Tough times don't last but tough people do. Consider this. Every tough circumstance you have in your life will become part of your success story. I once heard someone say "Until you handle it with grace, It will stay in your face"....now with that said just let that sink in

Being laid off is one of the most demoralizing experiences anyone can ever have. Trust me I have been laid off twice in one year. The disappointment and reality of knowing your source of income is gone is really traumatizing. When it happened to me though disappointed I came to realize that it was the best thing to occur for me. I got out of a negative environment and my mindset changed and I began to start not just seeking opportunities but also creating opportunities for my life. Eventually I got not just better employment but I got better opportunities. It was like a fire was lit under me and I sent out over 300 applications. I learned something, sometimes it takes for all the chips to be down in order for one to get up and get moving. The road to success is bumpy but once you put the rubber to the road, combine with optimism, all obstacles can be overcome.... Now with that said just let that sink in.

You are the summary of your thoughts. No surprises here. You are where you are in life because of your thoughts. You can't blame anything on anyone. What you think of yourself is reflected in your habits, speech, occupation, interactions and relationships. James Allen author of "As a Man Thinketh" illustrates why people are where they are in life ... "Men are anxious to improve their circumstances but unwilling to improve themselves; they therefore remain bound". If you refuse to improve the things you can control then how can you change your circumstances? Changing your thoughts and how you see and accept things is key to changing your circumstances. Yes unfortunately, bad situations occur however, I have the utmost belief that most situations can be turned around and aren't impossible to overcome. That process must start via your thoughts.........now with that said just let that sink in

Being negative will get you know where quickly. Negativity has no gains so why waste your time doing something that produces nothing. Always remember that a person who only sees the downside of life is a person that emits the wrong kind of energy. What you exhibit to yourself is what you will display to the world. Every single day you wake up you should set your thoughts and action towards positivity. Clothe your heart, mind and soul with the idea of positivity. Being positive is the most uplifting thing you can do for yourself.........now with that said just let that sink in.

Anytime you go against the status quo you are deemed disrespectful. However, all the greats have that in common Ali, Gandhi, Mandela, MLK, Malcolm X, Lincoln, Marcus Garvey, etc..... The good thing is that history has exonerated them and they are now viewed as inspirational figures that stood up for what they believed in regardless of how inappropriate it was. Standing up for what is right is better than fitting into the system. Make no excuses or arguments in favor of societies wrongs just to maintain the status quo.... now with that said just let that sink

No matter what you do in life there will always be someone eager to play the role of antagonist. Someone constantly mirroring your every move seeking to turn your positive into a negative. Today I tell you continue to focus on the progress and good work you are doing. If that person wants to relegate themselves to the level of a distraction in your life, it is absolutely none of your business. Be like a failed chemistry experiment and offer them no reaction...... now with that said just let that sink in

A fundamental problem I notice everyday is that the majority of individuals, businesses, educational institutions and Politicians play a game which renowned Radio personality and speaker Earl Nightingale called "follow the Follower". It simply states that instead of modeling one's self/business/organization on the one exception model everyone pretty much plays copycat and just tries to fit into a model already in place. By endorsing that philosophy pretty much you would guarantee mediocrity in whatever pursuits you seek. Look at all the successful business/people in this world and realize they didn't fit the mold but they broke the mold. You are a leader and you know it. Great Leaders don't play "Follow the Follower" but they seek to be the exception in everything that they do….. Now with that said just let that sink in

Venomous snakes are some of the most deadly creatures in the world and people around the world fear them and with good cause. In sacs located in their upper jaw these snakes contain toxins aka venom from which they bite/inject into their victim or any living thing perceived to be a threat. Some of these toxins can kill within 15 minutes. However scientific research and technological advancement have allowed mankind to benefit from a cure aka Anti-venom. The antivenom in a nutshell is a breaking down of the venom and creating antibodies thus providing immunity to neutralize the effects of toxins. Lesson learned here is that researchers took a negative and turned it into a positive. Same way in our daily encounters we too can turn negatives into positives by using a little ingenuity and patience. There is an old saying when life hands you lemons make lemonade. These scientists certainly applied this and I hope and believe you will also......now with that said just let that sink in

When I first started driving I was very nervous about everything I did while driving. One might even say that I was fearful at doing basic maneuvers as overtaking, switching lanes, reversing, etc...In some instance I would even stay behind a slow moving vehicle just to avoid having to do anything out of the ordinary. Sometimes I would take the local roads which were much slower than take the highway all out of fear. Eventually one day I asked myself, what am I afraid of and started to build up my confidence to confront my fears. Gradually if my memory serves me well within two weeks I was driving on the highways and performing all basic driving maneuvers with confidence. My point is until you confront your fears you will always be limited in you capacity. Fears are most of the times based on our perceptions which are illusions in our minds. When we confront our fears and move past them it becomes a vital learning experience. Don't live (or in my case drive) within your fears….. Now with that said just let that sink in

There is a misconception that a lot of people have. They base their knowledge on their education level alone. They believe that their opinion of things holds more weight because of education. The problem with this is, if you rely on your education for "knowledge" you will always be stuck on that level. What I try to practice is not to be educated alone but to be learned. Do your own researches, read materials outside of a syllabus, ask questions from experienced individuals and pay attention to current affairs. Ask any extremely successful person in their field what separated them from the rest of their colleagues and they will tell you they expanded their learning pass their education. While I always recommend higher education pursuits even more than that I endorse learning outside of the classroom. It is always better to learn and be informed than to just simply be the holder of a degree. Education is limited but learning expands your mind and your life ….now with that said just let that sink in

I learned that a company growing at a rate of 10% a year cans double its efficiency within 8 years. However, if a man invests in himself, he can increase his own efficiency to 100% in one year. When asked by reporters what is the greatest investment one can make, Business mogul Warren Buffet replied" Investing in themselves". Read, listen, ask questions, research, seek counsel etc… When you invest in yourself you give yourself an extra advantage in life. It is your life so why won't you at least invest in it……now with that said just let that sink in

Something I realized which impacted my very existence is that every time I allow a negative thought to manipulate my thinking and actions I never yielded the results I wanted only the result I expected. I have never gained anything by believing in my own negative thoughts. Until I realized all I had to do was combine positive thoughts with positive action. William James the Famous American Philosopher and psychologist, also the first person to offer a course on psychology in the United States once said" The greatest discovery of my generation is that a human being can alter his life by altering his attitude". Pretty much we get and become what we think about. Today I encourage you to immerse your mind in positivity and soon enough the results will follow. When you think positive, you will act positive and you will yield positive results…. now with that said just let that sink in

Samuel Langhorne Clemens is a man who went through many troubles. First he was born at a time when childhood/infancy deaths were extremely high. At age 11 his father died of pneumonia and the year after Samuel dropped out of school in the 5th grade. Also he had some failed business ventures and bankruptcy. However, he had high hopes of being a writer and he continued to work steadfastly and worked many places and jobs such as a printer, typesetter, and silver miner and until finally a journalist in 1864. The next year he experienced his first success as a writer when he wrote the humorous tale "The Celebrated Jumping Frog of Calaveras County". Samuel decided that he would use a pen name and today you know him as famous Mark Twain the writer of such world renowned classics as "Huckleberry Finn" and "The Adventures of" Tom Sawyer". Now he was travelling around the world to lecture in places like Australia, New Zealand, Sri Lanka, Fiji etc…Lesson here is, dream big regardless of your challenges. Set goals and work towards them. They're your goal/dreams and only you can make them happen… now with that said just let that sink in

Your thinking is a reflection of who you really are. Your mindset holds the key as to whether you will be successful or not. Archibald MacLeish the Pulitzer award winning poet wrote in his play THE SECRET OF FREEDOM" The only thing about a man that is a man is his mind, everything else you can find on a pig or a horse". The funniest but most accurate statement I have ever heard. Animals don't think about success. Humans do. Your mindset will determine whether you live a life focused on basic subsistence or a life of superlative excellence. Your mind is more complex than an animal therefore your thought processes should be of a higher level. The key to your success is your mind. Improve your mind and I guarantee you will improve your life…. now with that said just let that sink in

Theodore Geisel was a man with big dreams who pursued his successes diligently. He was accepted in the Famed Oxford University but unfortunately left without attaining any degree. He then tried doing illustrations about his time in Europe which was rejected by Life magazine. Eventually one of his cartoons which were bought for $25 was featured in the July 16th 1927 issue of "The Saturday Evening Post". Later that year he accepted a job at a humor magazine's "Judge" as a writer and illustrator. He adopted the pen name "Dr. Suess' and the rest is history. From advertising campaigns for major companies to expanding into children books and cartoons selling over 600 million worldwide, 20 languages and net worth of over $75 million his works have become legendary. Notice he didn't allow his failures to stop his dream but rather he continued pressing on until his dream was realized. Remember failures are just Potholes on the road to success … now with that said just let that sink in

Let's embrace the idea of thinking futuristically. In other words what I am saying is I want you to start thinking ahead. When you embrace this concept you have an end product in mind. You will be beginning to set goals and having a reason behind everything you do. You will have lesser extemporaneous decisions but you will be on a precise course with a precise goal. Planning is never overrated. Zig ziglar once said "You were born to win, but to be a winner; you must plan to win, prepare to win, and expect to win." Always think ahead. Those futuristic thinkers are always the ones negate through the following recessions, bankruptcies, loss of income and even experience financial success when the markets deem it impossible. Thinking ahead allows you to stay front of the competition without competing with them but by creating for yourself. I encourage everyone to always think ahead… it makes life easier and better. …now with that said just let that sink in

In order to succeed and realize your greatness you cannot be a common thinker. You cannot be restrained by the commonality of life. You must not participate in the rat race of life. You have to make difficult choices and decisions when it comes to your thinking, habits and ultimately your lifestyle. It is ok to have million dollar dreams with five dollars in your pocket as long as you have a million dollar mentality. Most people can think in terms of the status quo. No successful person has got success by going along with the flow. Empty pockets don't hold back people only empty heads do ……. Now with that said just let that sink in

In economics there is something called Opportunity Cost which is defined as the loss or potential gain from other alternatives when one alternative is chosen? Every decision in life has an opportunity cost. The man who opts to read gains knowledge but loses out on the great party that was occurring while he was reading. Pretty much opportunity cost is whichever decision you make something will be sacrificed. It is up to you in life to decide what is worth losing and what is worth gaining. Weigh up you options in life because you may not see it in the short run but in the long term your opportunity cost may make or break you and you have to live with it…. Now with that said just let that sink in

Salmon run is when the salmon swim from the ocean into rivers heading upstream back to the place which they were born. Now this is not an easy feat for them. Many dangers await them in these rivers. Predators such as eagles, grizzly bears and even fisherman lay in wait to make a meal of them. Why do it? It is their biological manifest destiny to return to the place they were born to reproduce and die. Point is that when you have a goal or dream to accomplish there will be hardships and challenges that do not mean you should give up on them. Swim against the current. Do like the salmon and don't be fazed by circumstances…….. Now with that said just let that sink in

One of my favorite biblical scriptures is found in Mark 9.23 (KJV) where Jesus said "If thou canst believe, all things are possible to him that believeth". A truly profound scripture and something that regardless of your religious/spiritual beliefs can be applied to anyone's lifestyle. When you believe in attaining a result you will be so motivated that you will be able to visualize it. Also belief causes one to work towards something until it is accomplished. Believing eventually equates to self actualization – the realization of a goal achieved. All the impossible task people said that could not be done were made possible via hard work and belief. I implore you today don't doubt –Believe...now with that said just let that sink in.

Sometimes in life we don't always get the ideal scenarios we want in life but I honestly believe in maintaining a positive attitude regardless. Once you are alive you will encounter Murphy Law which states "Any that can go wrong, will go wrong" and I add to it at the worst possible time for it to go wrong. When things go wrong it is an opportunity to become an innovator of a solution rather than a complainer. Zig ziglar was once heard saying "Expect the best. Prepare for the worst. Capitalize on what comes". Pretty much it would equate to the old adage when life gives you lemons make lemonade. All the greats and successful people know that situations may never be ideal but it is your attitude within it that will ultimately determine if you advance or retrogress in life…. now with that said just let that sink in.

I hear a lot of people talk about not having enough time to pursue the things that they will like. Allow me to share how I create more time for myself. One of my passions is that I love to read. I already know that my day is going to be so jammed packed that if I don't create the time I won't have the time. Most mornings I try to get up at least an hour earlier when everyone is sleeping and devout myself to reading whatever material I deem necessary for myself development. Now simply by doing this only five days a week I just created six and a half extra 40 hour work weeks a year. Some people may complain that it is impossible because they have responsibilities, children and other things to take care of and that it is hard. At first it was hard for me but now it is easy. One of my favorite sayings is "if you do what is easy your life will be hard but if you do what is hard your life will be easy."… Now what that said just let that sink in

What you do with your free time plays a part in how successful you are. According to famous Speaker Earl Nightgale we have what he called discretionary hours where pretty much is the hours which we are neither working nor sleeping. However you choose to use them is up to you. I always encourage we can use some of these hours for self development. Example instead of playing videos for 4 hours we can split the time up 50-50. Two hours studying anything that interest you and 2 hours of playing video games. What you do in your discretionary hours can give you the edge over the playing field. The less time you spend on non essential activities in your free time the more time you will have to devout to improving yourself. Therefore if you want to get better at anything give it more of your free time and I promise you will reap the results...... now what that said just let that sink in

Too many of us are afraid to go after our dreams because it will require us to go against the status quo. We are fearful to dare to be different. Therefore most of us will accept and live in mediocrity just to conform. Existential psychologist Rollo May once stated "The opposite of courage in our society is not cowardice, it is conformity". Fear and conformity have held back more people than any other obstacle. Everything you want and desire is on the other side of fear. For those that love to conform let me leave you with this Earl Nightgale quote "Our rewards in life will be equal to our contribution". Excellence has never been associated with conformity...... now what that said just let that sink in

Made in the USA
Middletown, DE
26 July 2018